AROUND the ISLAND

Around the Island

Britain in a hundred days

Stan Lester

Avista

Published 2007 by Avista Press
96 Stoke Road
Taunton TA1 3EL
United Kingdom

A CIP catalogue record for this book is available from the British Library.

Printed and bound by Antony Rowe Limited, Eastbourne.

ISBN 978 0 9555441 0 1

To Phil, Anna, Chris, Ian, and Abi
and Janine who missed the voyage but checked the manuscript

Front cover: Ardnamurchan Point. *Stan Lester 2005.*
Back cover: Ardglass. *Stan Lester 2005.*

Contents

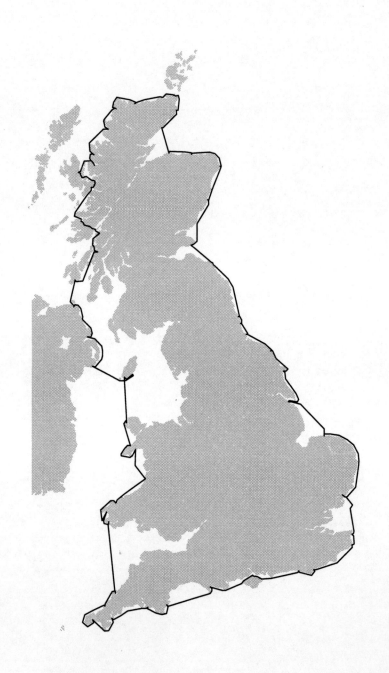

Prelude

Eight hours out from Fowey I was level with Start Point, and I steered *Indalo* just north of northeast to make the run across Start Bay. The wind had picked up from the southwest and at last I was making progress under sail, helming attentively in the swell to keep the breeze on the right side of the mainsail. I scanned the long sweep of the bay and beyond it the cliffs where the entrance to the River Dart, my home port, lay hidden. The drizzle had stopped and visibility was good though the sky was still overcast. With the wind behind me it felt warmer, and as soon as I was in calmer water I took off my coat, re-buckled my lifejacket and settled down on the edge of the cockpit to steer across the bay.

It was a Monday in mid-August and I was on my way back from Penzance after calling off an attempt to get to the Scilly Isles single-handed. I'd given myself a fortnight for the three-hundred-mile round trip, plenty of time but for the weather. The Atlantic seaboard had picked up the tail end of Hurricane Charley and I'd lost three days to gales. When they cleared I could have sailed over to the islands, spent a day there and got back to Cornwall, but then I would have been holed up in Penzance or Falmouth for the next week. Instead I decided to run for home. I'd already spent three weeks that year in brilliant weather cruising the Channel Islands and the Normandy coast, so I couldn't complain. Still, as I entered the Dart I felt disappointed to have had to backtrack without reaching the islands.

As I trickled up the river towards my mooring a thought began to take shape. What if I didn't have to turn back, and how long would it take to sail all the way around?

1

A Passage to Penzance

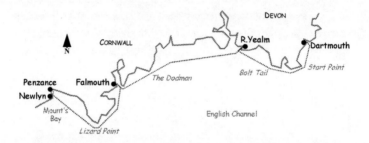

To sail around Britain in passages of not more than sixty miles, see something of the ports and anchorages on the way, and allow for the fickleness of the weather takes most people who attempt the voyage between two and five months. Settling on three and a half as a good average I could just fit it in if I set out by the middle of May. Once Christmas and New Year were out of the way I cleared my diary for the summer and drew up a rough voyage plan. Then I started making my preparations in earnest: I recruited my crew, stocked up on charts and pilot books, had some serious maintenance done on *Indalo*'s hull and rigging, updated her electronics and bought a windvane self-steering system. As the weather started to warm up I spent a couple of weekends fitting *Indalo* out and another off Dartmouth testing my new kit. By the end of April I was as ready as I ever would be.

The voyage began on the middle Saturday of May, a cold, grey day that belonged more to winter than to spring. On the way to the quay the mid-morning temperature struggled to reach a mere seven degrees, and as I transferred my bags on to the open ferry-cum-water-taxi that would take me out to *Indalo* the rain started in earnest. When we reached the moored yacht I paid the boatman, bundled everything down the mainhatch, followed it in and slid the cover over just as the skies opened. I sorted out the sodden bags to the sound of water hammering on the deck and wondered if this would be the pattern for the days to come. My luggage was dry, but enough water had come in with the bags and with me to make the cabin decidedly humid. I took off my foul-weather clothes carefully to avoid dripping on the bunks, then put my gear away: food and drink into the galley locker and under one of the spare berths, clothes in clear plastic bags on a hammock rigged over my bunk in the forecabin, computer in a padded bag, navigational things in the chart table, and everything else in a dry locker underneath my berth.

While the downpour carried on outside I studied my charts for the first stage of the voyage. The idea was to set off on Sunday around the southern tip of Devon and pick up a buoy in the River Yealm just east of Plymouth. If all went well I would take two more hops as the weather permitted to get to Penzance, from where I could head off to the Scilly Isles before turning north-east to rendezvous with my first crew at Padstow. I'd given myself two weeks to reach the north Cornish port, mainly to allow for bad weather but also in the hope of spending a few days in Scilly in compensation for my thwarted attempt the summer before.

By mid-afternoon there was a slight break in the rain so I slid the hatch open and went out to prepare *Indalo* for sailing. Kit such as lifebuoys, man-overboard marker, liferaft and self-steering windvane are kept below when the boat isn't being used, but now I was aboard they would stay in position above deck for the rest of the trip. Other jobs that needed doing included taking the sail cover off, untying various ropes and tying or clipping others on, and putting out the flags: British red ensign at the stern, green-and-white Devon flag on the port or left-hand side of the rigging, and to starboard an RNLI flag that would stay in place until I crossed over the Tamar into Cornwall and swapped it for St Piran's Cross, white on black. Finally to save myself a job when I arrived downriver I put out mooring ropes and fenders ready to tie up in Dartmouth.

With everything set up I started the engine, checked that I had fore and aft propulsion, and set off. As I passed back around the quay the rain returned with a vengeance. I'd only donned my lightweight waterproofs and hadn't bothered to put my boots on, so in a few minutes the water running down my trouser legs had filled my shoes. More water began to get up my sleeves and down my neck. Half an hour later I tied up and the downpour promptly stopped, but I was already squelching, bedraggled and in need of a change of clothes. Not a good start: next time, kit up properly.

I'd arranged to meet some friends from Torquay for the evening, which also happened to be the main night of the Dartmouth music festival. Declan I'd met a few years back when I was a novice doing a Competent Crew course and he was on the third rung up taking Coastal Skipper. We'd joined a sailing school yacht called *D'Artagnan* early in the evening and, after a brief discussion in the Dartmouth Arms over a couple of pints and a pizza, we voted to cross over to France. Immediately. So we drank up, the skipper worked out a course to steer, and we set off for Alderney. My dinner stayed down for about ten miles, though I did manage to do my stints at the helm. The following year when I bought *Indalo* Dec also came with me for my first tentative potter around Poole Harbour, and since then he and partner Brenda have been regular crew members. They couldn't join me on my voyage, but it was good to have them see me off.

4

The small town of Dartmouth is a classic West Country port, with a half-hidden entrance between high cliffs that widens out into a busy, deep and stunningly beautiful river-harbour. Its maritime history is decidedly colourful too. It's from here that the British fleet left for the Second Crusade in 1147, calling in on their way to help King Alfonso of Portugal capture Lisbon from the Moors. A smaller fleet joined the Third Crusade a few decades later, and in the fourteenth century the town provided ships and men for the siege of Calais. Like many West Country ports it was a base for pirates and privateers who harassed shipping and made raids on the French coast. One of the best known – there's a display about him in the castle near the river-mouth – is John Hawley, a merchant who conducted several raids on Normandy and Brittany. He once captured thirty-four ships and brought back so much wine that the streets were said to have run red with it. He also built the first of Dartmouth's three castles to pre-empt French reprisals, though it didn't stop Breton raiders from sacking much of the town a few years later. Hawley seems to have attracted equal amounts of approval and approbation, his career including a short spell in prison for taking a neutral ship and a somewhat longer one as mayor of Dartmouth.

Nowadays the most instantly recognisable name associated with the Dart is probably Agatha Christie, creator of Hercule Poirot and Miss Marple, who lived and wrote at Greenway House just back from where *Indalo* has her berth. The estate belongs to the National Trust and boat trips to see where she lived are advertised on the quay in Dartmouth. Strangely given the town's maritime heritage its links with two noted Elizabethan explorers go virtually unmentioned anywhere the casual visitor might look. Sir Humphrey Gilbert, the half-brother of Sir Walter Raleigh, was born at Greenway in 1539 and spent much of his life there. According to one version of the tale it was at his house that the pipe-smoking Raleigh was doused with water by a servant who thought he was on fire. Gilbert's own claim to fame was that he took possession of Newfoundland for the Queen in 1583; later his ship the *Squirrel* went down with all hands, Gilbert included, off the Azores.

The other local explorer and navigator was Captain John Davis, who hailed from Sandridge a mile or across the river from Greenway. A great navigator and a humane commander by the standards of his day, I've always regarded him as something of a sixteenth-century Captain Cook. Davis set out from Dartmouth in 1585 with two small ships called the *Sunshine* and the *Moonshine* to find the fabled Northwest Passage, the supposed sea route to the Orient via the north of Canada. He failed to find a route through to the Pacific – that had to wait for the Norwegian polar explorer Roald Amundsen over three centuries later – but he did find the entrance to Baffin Bay and sailed further north than any British navigator before him. He led two further voyages to the northwest (Davis Strait is named after him), commanded a ship against the Spanish armada, and explored the south Atlantic down to the Falklands, an arduous voyage where he lost two-thirds of his crew. Finally he turned his experience to piloting merchant fleets to what is now Indonesia in search of pepper, paving the way for British and Dutch merchantmen to challenge the Portuguese monopoly. Davis was killed in 1605 in a fight with Japanese pirates off Bintan, near Malacca. He wrote two books on navigation and exploration and invented a navigational device called the quadrant, the forerunner of today's sextant. Cutting a somewhat pious and academic figure for a sea-captain Davis has been over-shadowed by the dash and daring of his contemporaries Drake and Raleigh. He deserves better recognition.

Returning to the town, Dartmouth has a deep and sheltered natural harbour with access in most weather conditions, ideal for a merchant, fishing and naval port. Nevertheless the problem of transporting goods through its steep hinterland stopped it becoming a major industrial port or naval base and the lack of a sandy beach counted against it as a 19th- or 20th-century seaside resort. What has happened is that the town has developed a rather unique character: through the Britannia Royal Naval College it is Britain's base for training officer recruits, the quarter-mile wide river is packed with boats of all shapes and sizes, and there's a wealth of history in the compact town centre. From the visitor's point of view it's all rather attractive and welcoming, and it provides a lively but civilised place to spend a weekend or a week. And it seems to work from the more mundane perspective as a town for living and working in. I like the place, and I can't think of many spots within half a day's drive that I'd rather have as my home port.

Enticing though the Dart is, the next day's task was to bid it farewell and make my way to an equally beautiful if more rural Devonian river a little over thirty miles away. Sunday's weather forecast was for a dry day and a gentle to fresh easterly wind, ideal for rounding Start Point and heading west. To make best use of the tides I needed to be off the Start around three in the afternoon, which would give me a fair stream almost all the way to the River Yealm. I would have the tide against me to begin with, but it's much weaker in Start Bay than it is from the Point westwards. So there was no hurry: I had a leisurely shower and a walk around Dartmouth, bought some supplies, and got talking to an American yachtsman who was about to sail back to New York by way of the Azores and Bermuda. I've wanted to visit the Azores ever since I discovered the other Portuguese Atlantic territory of Madeira, so I was slightly envious. We parted with the sailor's farewell of fair winds and calm seas and I wandered back to *Indalo* to prepare for my first passage.

Slipping my ropes a few minutes before one o'clock, I motored off the Town Quay and passed between the twin forts guarding the river mouth. At last I had the feeling of setting off on a long-awaited adventure: the months of planning and preparation had come together and I was under way. The whole journey was ahead of me, both places familiar and those I could only imagine. For a moment it felt as if I had passed through an invisible boundary into a realm where everything was new, even the waters of Start Bay that I'd traversed regularly over the past five years.

The day was overcast and chilly, but at least it was dry and visibility was good. I had the wind on the beam or side of the boat where it's easiest to get the best from it, so progress was swift. The only problem with an easterly off Dartmouth is that the wind has half the length of the English Channel to raise a swell. Today the sea was what's described in the forecasts as 'moderate,' which means waves of around two metres between crest and trough. In a small yacht like *Indalo* that can be enough to make the boat roll uncomfortably, and by the time I reached Start Point I was beginning to feel slightly queasy: not enough to make me switch on my anti-seasickness device or take a pill, but just enough to tempt me to indulge in my favourite stomach-filler of a cheese roll helped down by some ginger beer.

As *Indalo* passed the Start I turned her westwards. The wind was now coming from behind, putting the boat on a dead run with the sails let right out. In theory this means the wind is simply pushing the yacht along, but what actually happens with a modern fore-and-aft rigged vessel is that the boat rolls from side to side, the foresail flaps around in the lee of the mainsail, and there's a risk of the wind getting on the wrong side of the sail and slamming it over in what's called an accidental gybe. Apart from the danger of damaging the rigging it doesn't do much for the heads of anyone caught in the way. A couple of years back in the Solent a yachtsman had been concussed and knocked overboard by a gybing sail, drowning before his less experienced shipmate could pick him up. It's a mishap to be avoided at any time, all the more when sailing single-handed.

The coastline from Start Point to Bolt Tail can look rather grim in the wrong light, but with even a glimmer of sun it's a stretch I always enjoy traversing. First comes the long neck of Start Point with its low lighthouse at the tip, then a broad reef-strewn sweep rising to the gnarled Prawle Point, the southernmost tip of Devon, that sports the rusty remains of a shipwreck on its rocks and a National Coastwatch lookout on the hill above. West of Prawle the cliffs become gentler and turn inland towards the shallow entrance to Salcombe, returning on the opposite side as the tall, sheer-bottomed hillsides of Bolt Head that provide shelter from the westerlies. Beyond, the four miles from Bolt Head to Bolt Tail is a dramatic stretch that's at its best on a sunny day when the reds, greys, blacks and greens of the cliffs present different aspects as they drift slowly past. Most of the Devon coast is gentle and hints of wide bays and shallow creeks, but this part is hard and unyielding, not a comfortable place to be when the weather picks up. Past the Tail the scene becomes softer once more as the cliffs recede past Hope Cove and the wide expanse of Bigbury Bay opens out.

As I passed abeam of Salcombe the wind dropped, so I swapped from sail power to the engine, set the autopilot for the Yealm estuary, sat back, and kept watch. Visibility had worsened over the last few miles and once I cleared Bolt Tail the shore rapidly receded from view, leaving little in the way of coastal features to claim my attention. Halfway across Bigbury Bay the monotony was broken by some gannets that had found a shoal of fish and were engaged in an aerial bombardment, each bird suddenly folding its wings to become a sleek and deadly arrow hurtling headlong into the water to snap up its unsuspecting prey. By the time the display had ended the shore was once more in view and there was less than an hour to go to my destination. As I closed with the coast I got out my hand compass to check I was clear of the offlying rocks, followed a bearing towards a church spire, and then turned to line up two markers on a hillside to clear some more rocks on the final approach. Making my way around an S-bend and through some moored boats I trickled into this magical river and tied up to an island pontoon for a quiet night away from the shore.

⚓

Monday was St Brendan's Day. Saint Brendan is the Irish abbot and navigator who reputedly made an epic voyage to America and back in the sixth century. The story of his wanderings, the *Navigatio*, reads like a seafaring myth akin to Homer's *Odyssey*, with tales of sea-monsters, columns of crystal and giants hurling molten rock. Strangely for an account of the travels of an Irish saint it contains a lot of practical detail about the voyage and not much about the miracles he would have been expected to perform, and that's what aroused the curiosity of explorer and writer Tim Severin and his historian wife Dorothy back in the 1970s. The Severins were convinced that the *Navigatio* was an account of a real sea-voyage and the more fantastic episodes were just contemporary ways of describing phenomena that sixth-century monks wouldn't have had explanations for: whales, icebergs, a volcanic eruption. Tim recruited leading experts and craftsmen to help him build a replica of the type of boat that St Brendan would have used, a curragh made of leather coverings fastened over a wooden frame, and with a small crew he made an epic journey of his own via the Faeroes, Iceland and Greenland to arrive in Newfoundland. This latter-day 'Brendan voyage' proved that the crossing could have been done with sixth-century technology and navigational techniques, and more than that it put modern names to some of the places (the 'paradise of birds,' the 'island of smiths') described in the *Navigatio*. The verdict can only be open, but Severin's voyage gives credence to Europeans reaching North America before Columbus and before the Vikings. More on this theme anon.

Back in the twenty-first century the weather forecast was for a light to moderate northwesterly wind and no rain, so I decided if not to cross the Atlantic then at least to push on further west. A late morning start was in order because it would use the tides as well as missing some naval gunnery practice that would be taking place just past the halfway point. So I spent the first part of the morning doing some chartwork and preparing my passage plan. Before starting a passage I make up some notes about where I'm going, the tides, the latest weather forecast, and what I need to look out for *en route* and when I'm entering port. I usually enter a route into the GPS, and when I'm sailing alone I make up some waterproof sketch plans and notes on laminated cards. These I keep in the cockpit clipped to a plastic chopping board purloined from the kitchen, so that if I need to I can do most of my navigating without going below. Also on my home-made clipboard is a log sheet for plotting my progress on the passage before transferring it to the ship's log at the end of the day.

Plans all done I set off just before eleven, the wind surprising me by coming from the southwest rather than the northwest as forecast. I hoisted the sails in the mouth of the Yealm, sailed across Plymouth Sound to the broad conical hill of Rame Head on the Cornish side, and then the wind dropped so I set a course under engine for my halfway point, a headland called the Dodman. A couple of hours later the wind picked up again now from the forecast direction, so the engine went off and I continued under sail. Just short of the Dodman I ran into the somewhat delayed gunnery practice. The frigate HMS *Westminster* steamed out of St Austell Bay, crossed close enough in front to make it wise for me to slow down, and fired an ear-splitting salvo at a target buoy in the distance.

If I'd sailed directly to Helford or Falmouth without calling in to the Yealm I would have passed close to the Eddystone Rocks, a hazardous reef about eleven miles south of Plymouth. From my more landward course the Eddystone lighthouse was visible only as a thin pencil on the horizon, but I mention it because it introduces a character who will make an appearance more than once on my journey. The present light was built by John Douglas in 1882 but the more famous one that now stands on Plymouth Hoe resplendent in red and white paint was the work of John Smeaton, a Yorkshireman from the Leeds area and one of the greatest of English maritime engineers. After starting to train in his father's profession of law he left to pursue his true vocation as an engineer. To begin with he concentrated on precision instruments, though he soon progressed to larger projects and his work on the Eddystone light paved the way for his success as a civil engineer. His light was built in 1759, the third attempt to establish a navigational signal on the Rocks. It stood for over a hundred years and would probably still be there today except that the particular rock it was on started to become unstable. When it was due to be replaced the light had found such a place in the hearts of locals that it was removed stone-by-stone and rebuilt in Plymouth.

Rounding the Dodman I still hadn't decided whether to head for Falmouth or Helford. Falmouth is a busy seaside and port town with fuel, marinas and plenty of places to eat. The Helford by contrast is an evocative rural river, a sister to the Yealm with a riverside inn and a welcoming yacht club, but the moorings are mid-river which means pumping up the dinghy to go ashore. I didn't need fuel and I'd decided to heat some tinned food to eat at sea, but as the decision-point loomed I felt in need of stretching my legs ashore and Falmouth beckoned. The town's visitor's marina also has some of the best showers in Cornwall and there's usually someone around who is willing to chat about their boat or their voyage over a drop of Madeira or a measure of Calvados. Turning into the estuary of the Fal I motored past the docks and approached the town at slow speed, spotting a vacant berth on one of the pontoons. I tied up, raised the Cornish flag, and went ashore for a walk and a drink.

Falmouth is Cornwall's main shipping port and it still has an active dock, a shipyard and a ferry terminal. For three hundred years until the end of the nineteenth century it had been one of England's busiest cargo ports. As well as being a popular unloading and revictualling station it was 'Falmouth for orders' – ships returning from distant lands would anchor off and await their owners' instructions about where to go to get the best price for their cargoes. For nearly two centuries it was the home of the Falmouth packets, fast-sailing post ships that took mail around the world, and it still has a fleet of sail-powered oyster dredgers. Nowadays the Fal is Cornwall's biggest sailing centre as any visit on a summer weekend will demonstrate. I'm not sure where it stands in relation to Dartmouth for single-handed circumnavigations (my home port can claim at least three), but two of the most important record-breaking voyages of recent times started and finished there. Sir Robin Knox-Johnston's was the first single-handed non-stop round-the-world voyage, which he completed in 1969 after 312 days in the eminently seaworthy but heavy and slow *Suhaili*, and Dame Ellen MacArthur's in 2004-5 set a new record at 71 days, 14 hours and 18 minutes in her purpose-built trimaran *B&Q/Castorama*.

An advantage of being in the Fal is that there are plenty of places to go if the weather isn't good for a seaward passage. On one of my previous cruises I spent a few days exploring the upper reaches, which for a boat of *Indalo*'s size extend to Truro. The quay is almost in the city centre, but it's not in the best of spots and involves drying (or rather oozing) out on soft mud. Truro is a small and in some respects rather fine cathedral city, but it doesn't take too much searching to find a run-down quality too. According to the Lester social index (based on the volume of litter, the number of shopping-trolleys in bodies of water, and the number of grossly overweight people hanging around smoking at the back of supermarkets) the city wasn't doing very well. Nevertheless by the time I had wandered into town and visited the indoor market, the cathedral precinct and a rather pleasant tea shop in what looked like an old church, Truro had redeemed itself somewhat.

This year the detour upriver would have been an indulgent luxury, but if the weather kept me in Falmouth I was looking forward to a visit to the newish National Maritime Museum. As it turned out the morning forecast was good for the passage west around the Lizard, and by the time I'd showered and bought some food there wasn't a lot of time left if I was to catch the tide. So I just had a chat with a neighbouring yachtsman whose boat I'd admired as I came in to the marina, and got ready to leave.

Lizard Point marks the end of the relatively benign southern Cornish coast with its easily-accessible and accommodating ports of refuge, and the beginning of Atlantic Cornwall where the wind can raise a fearsome sea against the cliffs and what ports there are can be difficult or impossible to enter with the waves in the wrong direction. The Lizard not only has strong tides that can kick up a dangerous sea in a blow, but it's strewn with rocks making an inshore passage foolhardy in anything but calm conditions. Naturally it's also littered with shipwrecks from the Manacles on the eastern side, just south of the entrance to the Helford River, right around to Mullion Cove to its west. Though its cliffs are a mere sixty metres high its granite bulk dominates a voyage for miles either side, whether westward-bound to Scilly or Mount's Bay or eastward to Fowey, Falmouth or up-channel. As the southernmost point of the British mainland it should take pride of place over Land's End, which is just another bump on a continuous stretch of cliffs and falls several miles short of being the island's westernmost tip. Nevertheless Land's End marks the extreme end of Cornwall and 'Lizard

Point to Dunnet Head' just doesn't work in quite the same way as 'Land's End to John O'Groats.'

My plan for getting around the Lizard was to arrive off the Manacles as the tide was beginning to slacken, and then carry a fair stream around the headland and across Mount's Bay. I got under way at half-past twelve and picked up an easterly breeze that had *Indalo* doing five and a half knots out of Falmouth harbour. At the mouth of the Helford the wind dropped to a whisper, so once more I put the engine on and motorsailed. I cleared the Lizard at four in the afternoon, logged the southernmost point of the voyage at 49° 56'.4 N, then set a straight-line course for Penzance. As I approached the western shore and looked back the sun was setting and Mount's Bay was lit up with a brilliant glow from the west. I had a dramatic view of St Michael's Mount, a rowing gig was silhouetted on the water in front of the cliffs, and the Isles of Scilly ferry *Scillonian III* stood out in splendid white against the dark clouds gathering to the east.

Penzance's inner harbour opens only an hour before high water so I planned to pick up one of the visitor's buoys outside and have a meal and a short rest before going in at midnight. But I couldn't find the buoys and ignoring the possibility of anchoring I moved to the all-tide harbour at Newlyn for the night. The downside of berthing in Newlyn is that it's a busy fishing port and the chances are that you will be tied up against a fishing boat, which is no problem until it needs to leave at first light. The best place I could find was on the outside of three boats that were all leaving between four and six in the morning. I supposed I deserved it for being too lazy to anchor. I decided to make the best of it and prepare a meal on board, then rather than having my sleep disturbed in the morning I'd move back to Penzance.

I like night sailing, but motoring single-handed close to the coast is nerve-racking because it's not easy to see what's in the water. The main hazards are lobster-pots, or rather the rope from the string of pots on the sea bed to the marker on the surface: if that gets wrapped around the propeller the boat is effectively disabled. Even large orange markers with tall flags attached aren't at all easy to see against the lights of the shore, and some fishermen still use five-litre oil cans that are all but invisible in the dark. So I treated the short passage as a proper sea voyage, donned lifejacket and harness, drew a pilotage plan with courses to steer and the lights I expected to see, and set a course for Penzance at little more than walking pace. I missed the lobster pots, entered the dock, and tied up next to a Dutch yacht called *Bloesem*, fifth boat out from the quay. It was nearing two in the morning when I'd secured everything, checked in with the harbour staff, and finally got into my sleeping bag. Whatever the weather held I decided that the crossing to the Scilly Isles could wait until Thursday.

2

Wind in the West

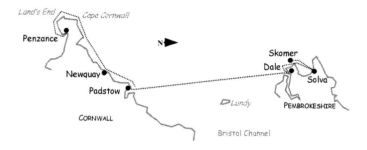

I like Penzance. It's the last proper town in England, the last stop on the Great Western Railway, and it still has an outpost feel tempered by a self-sufficient charm and the knowledge that the railway and the A30 are there if you need them. Because of that it's hard to categorise the place. There's a fair amount of gift-wrapped Cornishness and low-key seaside tat, but it's obviously not just a holiday resort and you don't have to scratch the surface too much to find a town for all seasons. The harbour takes up most of the northern end of the sea front, and though Penzance is the main ferry and cargo terminal for the Scilly Isles it's not a major trading or fishing port. There's still a small but healthy ship and boat repair industry, and the dock is home to an eclectic mix of coasters and fishing boats, long-distance and liveaboard yachts, long-term refits, a floating shop, the odd historic sailing boat doing trips and charters, and the chunky cargo ship *Gry Maritha* that takes up the whole of one side of the quay when it comes in to load up with cargo for Scilly. Take a walk inland through the side streets and it's not difficult to find the arty and alternative aspects of Pen Sans, the Holy Headland, though it's neither as arty as St Ives nor as alternative as Totnes.

Though Wednesday was fair the forecast for the next two days was for strong winds and rough seas from the west, so I resigned myself to staying put until the weekend. I'd been into Penzance harbour several times on passage and it wasn't unusual to have to wait for a day or two for the weather to improve. At least I could do some jobs around the boat and stock up on provisions. Most of the shops are in Market Jew Street, which I'd mistakenly imagined was named after its mediaeval traders; it's simply from the Cornish for Thursday (*yow*), Penzance's market day. Shopping completed I wandered back to the harbour and had another of my linguistic assumptions corrected, this time about *Gry Maritha*. Rather embarrassingly I asked what the name meant in Cornish, to be told that the ship was simply named after the daughter of her first owner, a Norwegian.

Something else I like about Penzance is that it's full of good watering-holes and places to eat. For the evening I chose a restaurant called the Sukothai that I can heartily recommend, then I strolled around the town and spotted the slightly old-fashioned, cosy Savoy cinema. I had some time to spare and liking old-style cinemas I checked to see if there was anything half-interesting showing. It was *Hitchhiker's Guide to the Galaxy*. The original radio series had something of a cult status in my student days and I still have a couple of the books, so I thought it was worth a look. After being left to my own imagination for so long (I'd only caught a brief snatch of the TV version) the film was disappointing, but it did capture some of Douglas Adams' humour quite well and it got the comically horrible Vogons off to a T.

Thursday was windy but mainly dry, not good for sailing around the tip of Cornwall but ideal for going into tourist mode. I took a double-decker bus out of town through woods and down flower-filled lanes, through a one-street village called Sheffield, on to St Buryan, and off at Porthcurno where I walked down the road to the Minack Theatre. This atmospheric place was carved out of the cliffside in 1932 by Rowena Cade, the daughter of a Derbyshire mill owner who had settled in Porthcurno a few years before and had a lifelong interest in stage sets and costumes. It became damaged and overgrown during the war, but afterwards Rowena with her gardener Billy Rawlings returned it to something like the condition it's in now. It's an impressive sight perched on the cliff-edge, better no doubt when a play is being staged there on a summer's evening. Even without anything going on it's worth a visit, and as well as the theatre itself the audio-visual display at the entrance is pleasantly informative and there's a neat little café with views over the coast and out to sea.

In the evening I strolled into town for a meal and found myself in Chapel Street, which has a choice of pubs, a tapas bar and an Indian restaurant. I went into the Union Hotel, unpretentious, roomy and welcoming, and it did a good fish pie *and* they knew how to cook vegetables properly. Formerly called the Ship and Castle, the hotel was old enough to have been attacked by some marauding Spaniards at the end of the sixteenth century and it was also the place where news of the victory at Trafalgar and of Nelson's death came to England two centuries ago. The messengers who arrived in the harbour found mayor Thomas Giddy at a ball in the hotel, where he made an official announcement on the spot. Before leaving the Union I spoke to an elderly gentleman who used to run the coastal radio station at Land's End and was in Penzance on holiday; our conversation had some relevance to a story I will shortly tell.

The night saw strong winds sweeping across the harbour, the noise rousing me at four in the morning to check all was well with the mooring ropes. Only an hour to go to the early-morning weather forecast, so I made a cup of tea and sat up

19

to wait. The news wasn't encouraging: there would be no let-up for the next three days, putting my departure back until Monday. I finished my tea, switched the alarm off, and curled up in my sleeping bag.

As the day wore on the sun came out and I decided to walk along the coast to Mousehole (which is pronounced 'Mouzle' and never in a way that suggests it's anything to do with small long-tailed creatures). On the way I wanted to take a look at a feature that I'd seen enough times from seaward but never visited from the shore. I followed the rather genteel southern promenade out of Penzance and continued through the working area of Newlyn, now the south-west's and very possibly England's busiest fishing port. There wasn't much activity at mid-day other than a man in overalls washing down a concrete apron outside some fish sheds, and a girl on the stony beach getting her big black retriever to retrieve an even bigger blue plastic oil drum. I watched them for a few minutes then I walked up the wide coast path out of Newlyn and found what I was looking for: the disused lifeboat station, now a memorial to the Penlee lifeboat disaster.

On 18th December 1981 the *Union Star*, a 1400 ton cargo ship registered in Dublin, was passing Cornwall on her maiden voyage to deliver fertiliser from Ijmuiden in the Netherlands to Arklow in Ireland. She was captained by Henry Morton with four crew plus wife Dawn and two teenage daughters. Eight miles east of Wolf Rock, the lonely lighthouse on the way to the Scilly Isles, she developed an engine fault in rough seas and put down her anchor. The next day she began to drag towards the rocks off Tater-Du a little further around the coast from Mousehole, and the captain put out a mayday call. The Penlee lifeboat, the *Solomon Browne*, was called out along with a helicopter from RNAS Culdrose on the Lizard. The helicopter couldn't get a line down to the stricken ship in the big sea so all depended on the lifeboat, now battling through forty-foot waves in hurricane-force conditions. Coxswain William Trevelyan Richards decided to close with the *Union Star*, but he had to make several attempts before getting alongside and twice the *Solomon Browne* was thrown on to the ship's deck. The lifeboat had already achieved the near-impossible and taken off four of the ship's complement when Trevelyan Richards decided to go in again for the rest. What happened next wasn't clear but ten minutes later the lifeboat's lights had disappeared and the *Union Star* keeled over with the loss of those still on board. The lifeboat's crew of eight and the four rescued from the *Union Star* also perished, leaving the local community in a state of shock. Every nineteenth of December Mousehole's famous Christmas lights are extinguished for an hour in the evening as a mark of respect and remembrance.

Now part of the conversation I had in the Union Hotel was about a trend for ship owners to become involved in operational decisions rather than leaving them to the captain. This, claimed my friend, was compromising safety and sometimes putting pressure on skippers to do their utmost to save vessels and cargos when the sensible decision would be to broadcast a mayday and leave the fate of the ship to the emergency services. I haven't come across any evidence to suggest this was a factor in the Penlee disaster, but I wonder if the outcome would have been any different had Captain Morton raised the alarm the day before.

A happier winter anniversary that's kept in Mousehole is Tom Bawcock's Eve four days later. Around two hundred years ago the little fishing port had suffered a series of tremendous storms, wrecking many of the boats and preventing the rest putting to sea. The village was close to exhausting its stocks of food and faced the prospect of Christmas on dwindling rations. In desperation a fisherman named Tom Bawcock set out on the day before Christmas Eve, his boat quickly disappearing out of sight among the massive waves. Just as the villagers were giving up hope for his return he reappeared in the tumultuous seas, struggling to bring his boat alongside and secure it to the quay. Tom landed a huge catch of seven types of fish, enough to keep the village from starving until the storms had died down. The day named after him is celebrated with a curious dish called Starry Gazy Pie, made from the seven kinds of fish that Tom caught all arranged with their heads poking through the pastry crust.

I walked into Mousehole itself and wandered around its attractive, fan-shaped harbour. With simple, sturdy walls, a rocky islet outside and traditional houses cascading down to the harbour's edge this is exactly what a Cornish fishing village should look like. It's incredibly busy in the summer and tourism has replaced fishing as the main source of income, though there's still a small fleet of boats. I called at the Ship Inn, in season the focus of the Tom Bawcock celebrations, and had a pint of a local beer called HSD or (and this is much more memorable than the real name) High-Speed Death. I checked the menu for Starry Gazy Pie, but evidently it's not in demand this time of year.

The next day I settled down to doing the navigation for the crossing to Scilly. A passage to be treated with respect, it involves entering into the open Atlantic with its ever-present swell and lack of a safe haven in a storm. Even so the distance of just under forty miles seems impossibly short to come to such an exotic and, well, different location. In sunny weather the main harbour on St Mary's is idyllic. Sitting in Juliet's Garden, a café-restaurant just outside the little capital of Hugh Town, the view sweeps across a glasshouse, around the tight curve of the boat-packed bay and on up to the sixteenth century Star Castle on the Hugh, a peninsula connected to the main island by a narrow strip of what's basically sand. To the right the off-islands sparkle in the distance and to the left the lower, middle part of Hugh Town straddles the isthmus as a thin line of houses on the strand. Behind them the land gives way to Porthcressa Bay and the open ocean beyond. The harbour is thronged with moored boats all pointing the same way into the breeze, and there's a gentle buzz of activity as someone rows ashore in a dinghy, a family play on the beach, a trip boat loads up with passengers. And that's just a part of one island. Tresco has a magnificent subtropical garden and long unspoilt beaches to match. St Agnes is a tiny community with a sheltered inlet on one side and a rocky coast exposed to the full fury of the Atlantic on the other. Bryher, opposite Tresco, is the most obviously English of the islands but it's an England that elsewhere passed away before I was born. The fifth island, St Martin's, I have yet to visit.

Scilly isn't a place to be in stormy weather, for though there's likely to be a safe haven somewhere it means moving around the islands to find a sheltered lee and then sitting at anchor ready to move as soon as the wind shifts. On Sunday the forecast took a turn for the worse and I reluctantly gave up the idea of making the crossing, planning instead to round Land's End, wait for the tide overnight at St Ives or Newquay, and head up to the next safe harbour at Padstow where I would meet Phil, my crew for the Bristol Channel. That was if I ever escaped from Penzance: the forecast was making it look doubtful for the whole of the next week. I was beginning to feel that I was trapped like Patrick McGoohan in the sixties TV series *The Prisoner*, with the swivelling lock-gate standing in for the bars that come down in front of his face at the end of each episode.

In the afternoon I did the navigation for Padstow, wiped the crossing to Scilly off my laminated cards, and to stop myself feeling too sad at having missed the islands two years in a row I found some small and unnecessary jobs to do on board like rearranging things in lockers and putting matching socks together. Before I could get on to pairing up underclothes my neighbour tapped on the hull and invited me on board *Bloesem*, where we shared some lamb chops and a bottle of wine. A retired Dutch doctor called Wolter, he had sailed over from the Somme with his brother and was about to continue on his own to Scotland. Larger than *Indalo*, his boat wasn't quite as roomy inside but she felt homely and well set up with leather seats, lots of wood, and oil lamps and stove. Built in Ijmuiden in 1960, she was an early example of a fibreglass-hulled yacht and turned out to be notably seaworthy; a similar boat called *Take Bora* had been sailed singlehandedly across the world by air force general Hans Maurenbrecher, eventually disappearing in a storm off the Great Barrier Reef. She was certainly an attractive little ship with twin masts, wooden spars and largely wooden topsides, and I suspected with her long keel and seakindly shape she would be rather more comfortable than *Indalo* in a heavy sea.

The next morning was just right for a walk eastwards along the beach to St Michael's Mount: breezy though not too cold, with the sun glittering on the waves. It was ideal too for the kitesurfers who were performing acrobatics between the beach and the Mount. The tide was still out when I arrived, so I walked across the beach and joined the causeway that links the island with the village of Marazion. After a quick lunch in the National Trust tearooms I climbed the winding path to the summit, taking in the panoramic views across Mount's Bay before making my way back to catch the ferry across the now-submerged causeway.

The Mount is a granite outcrop in an otherwise gentle stretch of coastline, and until the advent of the bubble-wrap of the Eden Project it was the most iconic and instantly-recognisable feature in the whole of Cornwall. Its harbour has probably been in use for over three and a half millennia and there's a first-century Greek account of an island called Ictis where tin streamers from Belerion (modern Penwith, the 'toe' of Cornwall) would carry their wares across a tidal causeway to trade with Phoenician merchants. Its modern name originated in 495 AD when some fishermen had a vision of St Michael on the Mount, though there doesn't seem to have been a place of worship there until Edward the Confessor allowed the monks of Mont St Michel in Normandy to build a chapel. A Benedictine priory was built around seventy years later, but from the time of King John until the end of the Civil War the Mount's military advantages have overshadowed its spiritual role. More recently it has enjoyed a peaceful existence as the home of the St Aubyn family, nowadays under the protection of the National Trust. It's a special and unique place, maybe not as atmospheric as its bigger French counterpart, but well worth a visit.

The following morning the weather was no better, though there was a hint that conditions might improve overnight. Continuing the tourist trail I walked inland to Trengwainton, a woodland garden just outside Penzance, and after a stroll around the grounds and another National Trust lunch I meandered back through the town realising I'd grown quite attached to it over the week of my enforced stay. Back on board I prepared for my departure, initially to Newlyn then around to Padstow if conditions were fair, into Mousehole for a change of scene if they weren't.

On *Bloesem* Wolter was getting ready to leave too and we adjourned to the Union Hotel to discuss our plans. He was intending to make the long crossing to Milford Haven, but after checking the distance and tides he thought better of it and opted like me to head for Padstow. It's important to get the timing right for a passage up the north Cornish coast both to catch a fair tide around Land's End and Cape Cornwall, and to arrive at Padstow close enough to high water to get into the harbour. We would need to leave Penzance early in the morning before the dock gate closed, wait about four hours before setting off, and then make another stop on the north coast while the tide went against us before doing the last stretch into port. The entire passage would take slightly more than twenty-four hours, so we needed a day or two of fair weather. In the wrong conditions Cornwall's northern seaboard can be totally bare of ports of refuge or safe anchorages, one of the most treacherous places on British shores; it's not somewhere to be when there's a gale coming in from the west.

On Wednesday I awoke to my mobile-phone alarm at five o'clock and immediately logged in to the Met Office website to check the weather. It was as good as we would be getting for the rest of the week with rough seas falling to moderate and a south or southwesterly moderate to fresh breeze, increasing to strong or near-gale later on Thursday. Perhaps a bit uncomfortable then, but not dangerous and there would be some shelter behind the headlands of St Ives or Newquay out of the wind and tide. I had a final shower in Penzance before saying farewell to the harbour at 0645, *Bloesem* following a few minutes behind for the short hop to Newlyn to wait for a fair tide.

We left Newlyn at a quarter past eleven in mist, setting a course to clear the rocks off Mousehole before tracking westwards around Tater-Du and the Runnel Stone towards Land's End. The sea was still quite rough – even *Bloesem* was pitching violently – but there was a moderate breeze from the south-west so we were able to make some progress by beating or zig-zagging under sail. With a more modern rig I could set a tighter course into the wind than *Bloesem* so I was soon in the lead. The Longships rocks loomed out of the mist west of Land's End, and after passing to seaward of them I altered course towards Cape Cornwall and the twin islets called the Brisons. The sea was slightly flatter now and the wind was on the beam letting *Indalo* stretch her legs: six knots through the water, plus two-and-a-half from the tide. *Bloesem* liked the conditions even more because she made perhaps an extra half-knot, catching up as we passed St Ives. Soon afterwards the wind dropped a little and I called for some assistance from the engine. For a second time I went ahead of my companion who was struggling on under sail, and by a quarter to eight in the evening I was at anchor in Newquay Bay. I had covered fifty-three miles in eight and a half hours: not a bad passage. *Bloesem* joined me, I brewed some tea and heated up a Penzance pasty for supper, then turned in for an early night.

Sometime after dark I was woken by Wolter banging on the hull. A harbour launch had called over to warn us that we would go aground at low tide if we stayed where we were. We were both sure we had done our anchoring calculations properly, but we decided to be cautious and move anyway. It wouldn't look very good for the insurance claim if we had ignored the harbourmaster's advice and the boats had got damaged by pounding on the sand, so we re-anchored in deeper water and rolled about in the swell. I slept fitfully before waking for the 0240 weather forecast, getting up a little after to leave on the morning's tide.

I motored out of Newquay in a light mist, a faint breeze and an uncomfortable swell. I must have been more asleep than awake because a couple of hours up the coast I ignored my own pilotage instructions and turned in for Padstow the wrong side of Stepper Point, wondering for a moment why I was heading for a sandy beach and not the open estuary of the River Camel. I soon corrected my mistake and had an easy run in to Padstow harbour, berthing on the north quay next to a rather scruffy yacht that had some mountain-bikes stowed just in the place where I needed to step on board. *Bloesem* came in a few minutes later and tied up behind me as I was heading for the shower.

In the afternoon the weather brightened and I took a walk along the coastal path. The route heads upwards and soon offers views across the river and back across the little town of Padstow, and now the tide had dropped the estuary looked very different with its golden dunes revealed. Past a war memorial and a little cove, and the path swung around to the left to overlook the Doom Bar at the river mouth. The Bar's ominous-sounding name is nothing more than a corruption of 'dune,' but it's appropriate both because the bar is a hazard to anyone trying to take a short-cut from the sea into the river, and because of the decline of Padstow as a port due to its silting (or sanding) up. There's a myth connected with this about a fisherman who killed a mermaid, in some versions by mistake and in others because she spurned his advances. Either way, with her dying breath she cursed the town to wither as the river became choked with sand.

The fortunes of Padstow have indeed changed several times over its long history. It was originally known as Lodenek, but St Petroc came ashore there from Ireland in a coracle around 520 AD and founded a priory: Petroc's Stow was soon shortened to Padstow. The village was sacked by the Vikings in the tenth century and the priory moved to Bodmin. After a period of obscurity Padstow recovered in the Middle Ages and grew to become an important trading, fishing and boatbuilding town until by Elizabethan times it was one of England's principal ports and the headquarters of the Lord Lieutenant of Cornwall, one Walter Raleigh. The harbour was a regular port of call for sizeable merchantmen, and in the nineteenth century it was a popular departure point for emigrants to Canada. Finally, Padstow had a major role to play in the Cornish pilchard industry, and a spotter or 'huer' was posted out by Stepper Point to watch the sea for shoals of fish and call out the fishing fleet: to 'hue and cry.'

The cargo ships using Padstow have long since been replaced by the railway (itself now gone) and the road, and while there's an active fishing fleet it doesn't fill the harbour any more. The inner harbour is partly given over to yachts and leisure boats, and tourism has become the little town's main industry. From my walk I returned to Padstow by its back door past the Elizabethan Prideaux Place and St Petroc's Church, and as I came into the centre I was greeted by a street plan showing the location of the eight establishments owned by celebrity chef Rick Stein. Stein's very conspicuous presence in the town has certainly put it on the map for seafood lovers, and now that his own flagship restaurant books up months in advance others have moved in to be part of the general effect. Becoming the gourmet capital of Cornwall doesn't seem to have done Padstow any harm and there are still pub meals and pasties to be had so it doesn't have to be an expensive port of call.

Phil was due to arrive on Friday evening. Originally I'd planned to set off on Saturday morning and anchor off the island of Lundy for the night, but another gale was forecast for Friday night and into the early hours of Saturday, making a delay prudent. The harbour would next open on Saturday evening meaning that even if the gale blew itself out we would be arriving at Lundy in the dark with a heavy swell running. My contingency plan was a Sunday night crossing directly to Dale at the mouth of the River Cleddau, the wide estuary where Milford Haven and Pembroke sit further upstream. I rang Phil and explained the situation, but he was still keen to come down on Friday. If things came to the worst we would go upriver and take a look at Wadebridge.

Next morning I spotted a near-neighbour on the south quay. *High Potential* is based three mooring-buoys away from *Indalo* in the River Dart, and I knew her owner Geoff as the instructor on my VHF radio course when I started sailing. She is a Contessa 26, a small, low-slung but exceptionally sea-worthy yacht inspired by the phenomenally successful Swedish Folkboat. Despite being slimmer and lighter than *Indalo* the Contessa has several circumnavigations to her credit including that of Tania Aebi, the youngest woman to sail (nearly) single-handedly around the world. When I was learning to sail I read Peter Hancock's trilogy about his adventures in *Kylie*, another Contessa that he sailed around Britain and Ireland before exploring the Mediterranean and Caribbean, crossing the Atlantic twice. I'd thought about buying one but decided its four-foot-something headroom wasn't really suitable for my six-foot-something frame. Geoff, who is shorter than me, was also intending to sail around Britain; he had reached Padstow over a week previously only to be frustrated by the same weather that had kept me in Penzance.

⚓

Phil was keen to get out to sea, so subject to the weather forecast we planned a direct crossing to Dale over Saturday night. I was also getting tired of being in Padstow. There's nothing wrong with it as a town but the quayside is where all the holidaymakers gather and being a bank holiday weekend there were lots of them milling about only a boat's width from *Indalo*. It was like being in a zoo on the wrong side of the bars, and I wanted to escape. The idea for Saturday was to take it easy and get some rest before the night crossing, but I had to put up with people eating their ice-creams ten feet above my head, an organ-grinder grinding away at the end of the quay, and the ever-present cry of "high-speed trips" to tempt people on to the motor boats that were doing tours of the estuary. Phil decided to go for a walk out to the headland instead. I dozed for a while then Geoff called in and we discussed the passage to the Cleddau. The forecast was for a moderate to rough sea decaying to slight, wind moderate to fresh westerly dropping to a gentle breeze, visibility good. The passage was on. All that was left was to make the final preparations and have something to eat. I prepared some sandwiches while Phil went ashore for fish and chips, a decision I suspected he might regret before the night was out.

We – that is *Indalo*, *Bloesem*, *High Potential* and another yacht all crossing to Dale, and my neighbour with the mountain bikes heading for Penzance or Falmouth – all left the harbour at twenty past eight in the evening. The passage started well and there was enough light to see the dreaded pot-buoys, but as soon as we cleared Stepper Point we were exposed to a heavy sea. Phil didn't look too comfortable, but with confidence in the forecast I told him that the sea was always rough off Padstow after a blow and it would calm down a little once we were in open water. I set the windvane self-steering gear and pointed us in the direction of the Cleddau, allowing for some leeway and tidal drift. Even if the passage was going to be less than pleasant it looked as if *Indalo* would sail herself across on her own.

The swell didn't calm down and Phil eventually lost his fish and chips around dusk. I suggested he got his head down, and after another half-hour of looking completely miserable he adjourned to the sea-berth, a small bunk that's rigged with a sailcloth to stop the occupant falling out when the boat rolls or heels. I wasn't feeling in the best form myself, but it was a light night with stars and moon out, and there were lights from other boats and from the shore to keep an eye on. Nevertheless it was surprisingly cold and I wasn't relishing the idea of keeping watch for the next twelve hours. At least *Indalo* was sailing at a respectable speed and in a straight line, so I didn't have anything energetic to do that might set off seasickness. Phil surprised me by re-appearing around three in the morning and offering to take over. I gratefully accepted, stretching out on the cabin floor in full kit and covering myself with an old sleeping-bag.

I came back on deck at half-past four much improved for my rest, and as soon as I'd reoriented myself Phil retired below. I'd missed daybreak which I'd been looking forward to, but I did witness a sunrise of sorts through the morning mist. The GPS was reading thirty miles to the next waypoint, about six hours to go until we came into the Cleddau, so we were over halfway. Other craft, yachts and oil tankers, started to appear on the horizon to add interest. Phil rejoined me around half-eight with land now in sight, and at last the sea began to settle to a lighter and more regular swell. A school of porpoises came out to meet us, by a quarter to ten we were entering the Cleddau and at 1130 we tied up to a pontoon off Dale, the sunniest spot in the whole of Wales. I replaced my Cornish cross with a Welsh dragon, and after a snack and a siesta we took the dinghy ashore to recover.

Our destination for Monday was Solva, a picturesque village on the north side of St Bride's Bay where Phil would depart by bus and train back to Bristol. To get to Solva we would either need to pass outside the islands of Skomer and Skokholm or brave the rapids in the bottleneck of Jack Sound that separates Skomer from the mainland. Either way (but particularly for the Jack Sound passage) getting the tides right is critical. So we left Dale at just after six in the morning and motored out of the river mouth in a flat-calm sea, ideal conditions for the Sound. Two other boats were ahead of us, so we could see if they had any difficulties; through my binoculars one of them looked like *High Potential*, and I watched her slow down against the tide to start with, then accelerate as it turned. Five minutes behind her we swept through the bottleneck and *Indalo* entered St Bride's Bay into a bright morning, calm sea and gentle breeze, the other yachts already on their way towards Ramsey Sound on the opposite side of the bay. I called up *High Potential* on the radio and Geoff confirmed he was bound for Fishguard. Crewed all the way and anxious to get on, he would soon leave me behind.

We hauled the sails up and made the rest of the passage at a gentle wind-powered speed, arriving off Solva just as the water became deep enough to get in. After making a careful entrance we picked up a mooring buoy and took the dinghy ashore for some lunch and a bus. Solva is an attractive spot and it was quite soporific sitting in the sun overlooking the harbour from the terrace of the boathouse café, but once Phil had left I decided not to linger but to return aboard and work out my passage plan for getting to Fishguard the next day. Doing the navigation I realised that there was a problem I'd not paid any attention to before now: catching the tide through Ramsey Sound and around St David's Head meant leaving near low water, which would be impossible if I was dried out in the shallow harbour. I needed to anchor in deeper water near the harbour mouth, and once the boat had grounded the next opportunity I'd get would be after dark when the rocks and reefs are hard to spot. Or I could do it now – *Indalo's* depth-sounder was reading zero, but she hadn't touched bottom yet. Leaving everything as it was I slipped the mooring and scraped out into the anchorage, a rocky pool of water close to the open sea.

There was a slight wind and a gentle swell coming directly into where I was anchored. I felt distinctly vulnerable, for if the wind picked up and the anchor dragged there would be only a couple of boat-lengths to go before I'd be on the rocks. It was too late to go back to the mooring, so I checked the chart for a less exposed deep-water anchorage. The most promising place was an inlet called North Haven on the bird-sanctuary island of Skomer, about eight miles across St Bride's Bay back in the direction we had come from. Without a moment to spare I crept carefully between the rocks and out of Solva, then piloted *Indalo* offshore and set the autohelm to steer for the north-eastern side of the island, donning fleece and lifejacket on passage. As I approached the haven I could see another yacht moored there, and there were two spare buoys marked 'day visitors.' I tied up to one of them and hoped they didn't mind night visitors. There were seabirds everywhere: puffins, guillemots and Manx shearwaters. Feeling immensely satisfied with the way my escape from Solva had worked out, I put the oven on for dinner and broke out a bottle of High-Speed Death while I reworked my passage plan for Fishguard.

3

Cymru

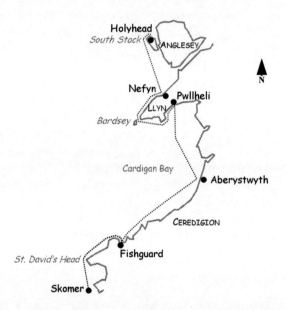

Tuesday began clear and bright on Skomer, not with the rain and drizzle that had been predicted. There was no wind and only a hint of a swell, so it looked to be a steady passage under engine to Fishguard. I slipped the mooring at nine and set a course across St Bride's Bay for Ramsey Sound, the short stretch of water between the mainland and Ramsey Island. When I arrived *Indalo* was met by the last of the south-going tide, but the stream soon turned and began to sweep me down the Sound. I kept a careful eye on my position to avoid being set on to the the jagged Bitches on the island side or the Horse lurking beneath the surface to landward. Followed by another yacht bound due north I was soon abeam of St David's Head, an ancient outcrop of lumpy granite that's one of the oldest exposed rock formations on the British coast. The sun was sparkling on the waves, the tide was with me and I sat back and let the engine and the autopilot do the work. I rang Anna, my next crew, to discuss meeting in Pwllheli on Saturday, watching the cliffs go past as we talked. A little later Strumble Head came into view and I changed over to manual steering as I thought there would be some disturbed water as the tide swept around the headland. Disturbed it wasn't, or by nothing more than some steep little wavelets, but the tide reached three, then four, then four-and-a-half knots. And it was only halfway up from neaps, the smallest of tides, to springs, the strongest. There's nothing in the pilot book or the Admiralty tidal atlas to warn of such a powerful current off Strumble Head, so I was glad I'd timed the passage to have it in my favour.

I turned into Fishguard in the early afternoon and headed across to the old fishing port, a harbour within a harbour, tying up against the wall ready to take the ground at low tide. The settlement around the old port is called Lower Fishguard and it's a rather attractive village though it seems to have no facilities other than two sailing clubs, both closed when I arrived. Wanting to stock up on groceries I crossed over a little bridge and walked up a steep and busy road to Upper Fishguard, the main town. I was out of ginger beer, my favourite drink on passage, but I couldn't find any anywhere and had to make do with fizzy orange instead. On the way back I followed my nose and discovered a quiet coastal footpath that skirted the back of the harbour and led down to the bridge, missing out the main road.

I wanted to stay on board *Indalo* until she had settled out on the bottom. By half-past six the keel nearest the quay had grounded on a lorry or tractor tyre, so as the tide dropped the boat heeled away from the wall. I wondered how to stop her from toppling over should the worst happen. I tied one of the halyards from the top of the mast to a big mooring ring on the quay, and did the same with a rope from a cleat on the far side of the deck. I sat and did some chart work, and waited. Eventually the second keel took the ground with the deck tilting at about twenty degrees, and I could leave *Indalo* in safety and go to the yacht club for a welcome shower.

There was nowhere to eat in the village so I walked back up to the town where I found an inn called the Royal Oak. A folk band was playing jigs and reels, the pub had a cosy, convivial atmosphere and the food and the beer were both excellent. A sign outside proclaimed that this is where the last invasion of Britain surrendered in 1797. Intrigued, I asked what the story was. An Irish-American general called William Tate had organised a small army of 1400 French mercenaries to attack Bristol, intending to divert attention from a larger French invasion planned to liberate Ireland. Bad weather forced them to land at Carregwastad Point, close to Fishguard, on 22nd February. Not knowing where they were and having nothing better to do, the invaders started looting the local villages. Before long a man called Tom Knox mobilised a group of volunteers to repel them, quickly joined by Lord Cawdor of Stackpole and his private yeomanry. Local cobbler Jemima Nichols rounded up twelve Frenchmen with a pitchfork. Two days after their arrival the invaders surrendered to Cawdor in the building that is now the Royal Oak. The invasion and its speedy defeat was commemorated on its bicentenary by the making of a 30-metre long tapestry, not alas on display in the pub.

The next day was the first of June, and I awoke at 0430 to a thoroughly wet Wednesday morning. The weather forecast was not too bad but not too good: wind up to a strong breeze or force six, and rain. I felt too tired to do a 65-mile passage in trying conditions so rather than setting off across Cardigan

Bay to Pwllheli, my next planned stop, I opted to move off the wall and anchor outside in the main harbour. It took less than half an hour to untie my ropes, get out and set the anchor, but there was a torrential downpour and I was soon soaked. After checking that the anchor was holding I retreated below, removed my wet clothes and got back into the sleeping bag to warm up.

I woke up for the second time at about half-past nine not looking forward to the prospect of a day anchored in the rain. It was too late to get to Pwllheli before nightfall, but a scan of the chart suggested Aberystwyth was a possibility. It's not the easiest port to enter in poor weather and I wanted to be sure of getting in because the only sensible alternative once there would be Abersoch, almost as far off as Pwllheli. I rang the harbourmaster for advice. He told me to arrive within two and a half hours of high water, but not to attempt an entry if there was much of a wind from the northwest. That meant I had until seven in the evening, giving me an hour to get ready and eight hours to complete the forty-mile passage. So there would be plenty of time with the wind behind me and the tide running northwards for all but the first two hours.

After making some quick preparations I upped anchor and was on my way at eleven. Now clad in dry clothes, full waterproofs and wellingtons I was impervious to the rain, and anyway it soon gave way to patchy drizzle and then to a general dampness under an overcast sky. The wind quickly dropped to moderate and then to a gentle breeze, barely enough to manage five knots in the rolling waves, so I put the engine on to make a respectable cruising speed. The swell though was still enough to defeat both the windvane and the electronic autopilot so I had to steer manually. At one o'clock I checked off the distance to go and with the tide turning in my favour I worked out I'd make port around six, well within the harbourmaster's limit for a safe entry.

By half past five I was off Aberystwyth. I turned into the waves to drop the mainsail before making a careful entry into

37

the harbour, *Indalo* rolling violently in the swell. There's a rocky ledge just before the entrance that has claimed at least one life in recent times, so it paid to be cautious. Nobody was answering the VHF radio so I found a clear spot where I could put out fenders and ropes and selected a free berth, tying up at six as I'd predicted.

The harbour is bordered on two sides by a rather soulless development of houses and office blocks and it didn't look particularly enticing in the grey of the evening. But I was safely ensconced in the marina, I had the next day off, and I could hope for things to look better in the sun. I took an evening stroll into town and got an impression of a lively place of many talents including plenty of restaurants and hostelries. After studying a few menus I found myself on North Parade (Rhodfa'r Gogledd in Welsh) and drawn towards the Agra, an atmospheric Indian establishment with sumptuous ruched ceilings and food to match.

⚓

Aberystwyth began to prosper when Edward 1 built a castle there in 1277, and it quickly established itself as a thriving fishing, boatbuilding and mining centre. After the railway arrived in Victorian times it expanded rapidly to become a fashionable holiday resort, the town centre getting a planned feel with some wide streets and grand terraces. This phase in its development extended the settlement north of the river Rheidol, the river that runs through the harbour, leaving the Ystwyth to play second fiddle on the southern edge of the town. It also confirmed Aberystwyth as a regional capital of sorts and a suitable location for national institutions: Aberystwyth University was founded in 1872 as the first college of the University of Wales, and in 1907 the town was selected as the site for the National Library of Wales.

Nowadays Aberystwyth has a population of a little over eleven thousand, swelled by seven thousand students in term-time and numerous visitors in the warmer months. Although that makes it a fair bit smaller than Penzance it's the hub for coastal mid-Wales and the only sizeable town in the region, giving it a compact shopping and commercial centre that's out of proportion to its size. It doesn't quite have the charm of the Cornish town and there are some fairly scruffy parts, but overall it's a confident and attractive place with the youngish feel of a university town to contrast with the mainly Victorian architecture. Unfortunately it's blighted by constant traffic queues, as the topography of the hinterland means that all north-to-south traffic is funnelled into the town centre. As I waited for what seemed an interminable time to cross the street I mused that Aberystwyth might benefit from some sympathetic Madeiran-style bridge and tunnel engineering to create a through road further up the valley.

On Thursday I set out to find out more about this heart of Welsh-speaking Wales. Calling in at the information centre for a street map I noticed that it's in what used to be the theatre, alongside the Ceredigion museum and art gallery. Inside the building is still set out like a theatre, as if it's only temporarily being used as a museum and one day the exhibits might be cleared away for a performance. The displays are housed in the auditorium and on two balcony terraces and themed so that there's some agricultural history, ship-building, domestic equipment and so on, as well as prehistoric and geological exhibits and a selection of paintings. I studied the maritime section and learned that the Ceredigion coast had once been a hive of shipbuilding activity, with an average of six ships a year built during the eighteenth and nineteenth centuries. The domestic exhibits included a few reminiscent of the kind of appliances I could remember from my childhood, but the thing that particularly caught my eye was a painted fire screen with a picture of an almost impossibly steep gorge spanned by a series of three bridges. Devil's Bridge, said the caption: does it really look like that or was some artistic licence being used, and could I get there by bus?

Leaving the museum I walked along the sea front promenade to a hill overlooking the north end of the town that had a funicular railway running to its summit. I bought a ticket and sat with a group of children in a rather dowdy carriage for my ride up the hill. In theory the ticket also provided admission to a Victorian *camera obscura* at the top, but the building was firmly closed, maybe permanently if the bars and locks on its door were anything to go by. The hill did though have some magnificent views over the town, the bay and the surrounding country, and if I'd not already eaten I could have had a cup of coffee and a bun in the café at the top. After walking around the summit in the wind I followed a meandering path back down, chatting on the way with some holidaymakers from the Midlands.

In the evening I wandered around the town centre to try to find a cosy pub for a meal, but with no success: I thought of the Union, the Turk's Head and the Admiral Benbow in Penzance, virtually next to each other. There are parts of Britain where pubs are for drinking and restaurants for eating, but I hadn't expect to find them so far south. I gave up for the moment and wandered around the part of town that contains the ruined castle and the church, then headed up to the station so I knew where it was in case I was still here on Saturday when Anna arrived. Part of the station concourse had been turned into a Wetherspoons called Yr Hen Orsaf. It wasn't the kind of pub I'd been hoping to find but the building was tastefully converted and while I was waiting for my food I got talking to two local women on an adjacent table who weren't conversing in Welsh. On my way out I stumbled across the terminus for the Vale of Rheidol Railway, which I couldn't help noticing was running steam trains to Pontarfynach, or in English the Devil's Bridge.

Friday awoke damp and overcast as well as windy, so rather than head up to the Devil's Bridge immediately I spent the morning in the National Library. The Library is housed in a big, imposing building on a hilltop to the east of the town, an edifice that wouldn't be out of place as a seat of government or presidential palace. It contains an immense collection of books, manuscripts, maps and photographs, and like the British Library it has the right to reserve a copy of everything that's published in the UK. I climbed the steps up to the grand entrance only to find a slightly dingy lobby with a small reception desk and some luggage lockers. I duly deposited my rucksack and set off to find whatever there was to be found. On the whole these big national libraries are not very interesting unless you are either looking for a book, researching something in particular, or there's an exhibition going on. At this one there were several, and the one that caught my eye was a photographic display called 'Aberfan: the days after' by New York photographer I C Rapoport. I'm old enough (just) to have a vague memory of the Aberfan disaster, or at least the discussions about it that went on for years afterwards. It happened on 21st October 1966 when a mountain of coal-slag collapsed on the village destroying the primary school and several houses and killing a hundred and forty-four people including 116 children. Rapoport arrived on the scene eight days later.

Reading the storyboard at the entrance to the exhibition I was unsure what to expect, as there's something ghoulish about turning up after a disaster and taking pictures of people many of whom had lost their children, loved ones, or whole families and hardly had time to come to terms with their grief or start rebuilding their lives. In fact the story that the exhibition told in pictures and in words was both sensitive and moving. I left feeling it was a fitting tribute to the dead, those who worked to rescue the survivors, and those who were left devastated by the tragedy.

The library also has a good buffet-restaurant, and I selected a bowl of cawl which I was disappointed to find out is just a word for soup, not Welsh lamb, leek and vegetable soup which was what I was expecting. Suitably warmed I collected my rucksack and took a muddy footpath back in the drizzle, heading for the Vale of Rheidol Railway and the afternoon train. Long after Dr Beeching's decimation of the branch lines and two decades after steam had given way to diesel and electric on the rest of the network the Rheidol line was still running as a steam railway within the British Rail system, passing to private ownership in 1989 and eventually to a charitable trust. (Beeching, whose decisions seem woefully shortsighted in retrospect, is curiously celebrated in the name of an Aberystwyth pub: perhaps given their escape from his proverbial axe the locals are having a joke at others' expense). I also noticed that the line is claimed to have the steepest gradient of any conventional railway in Britain, which probably explains why the trains go no faster than a steady trot.

I bought my ticket and clambered aboard the 1430 to Pontarfynach. The carriages were fairly basic with wooden bench seats and low, hard backs, but they were smartly painted and had all the original features like leather strops to open and close the windows. I shared a compartment with a large Welsh-Asian family, the mother including me in a distribution of some fruit that she had in a bag as an apology for the energetic behaviour of some of her children. The journey started off innocuously enough with the train pulling out of Aberystwyth station and passing through an area of suburbs and light industry at a steady pace, punctuated by the odd whistle as it approached crossing points and road junctions. It soon emerged into a landscape of rolling pasture, the hills either side gradually steepening. The locomotive chuffed its way up the side of the Rheidol valley, views across the hills opening up here and there between the vegetation. After a stop at Aberffwrd the excitement began, the track clinging to the side of steep, sometimes precipitous slopes with the valley floor perhaps a hundred metres below. The river widened out into a reservoir, the gradient increased and the train slowed almost to walking pace. Finally the track cut through a series of small gorges before levelling out for the Devil's Bridge terminus, where we got off in light drizzle.

Pontarfynach seemed little more than a cluster of cafés and tourist shops with the odd house dotted here and there. The bridge itself was a short walk away, and entering through a £1 turnstile I walked down some steps to a viewing point below the road and above some cauldrons formed by the river. The gorge was as steep as the painting in the museum suggested, but whereas I'd got an impression of three separate crossings telescoped by artistic licence, the bridges were actually built one on top of the other. The first of them was constructed by monks in the eleventh century, but its name comes from a legend that goes something like this. An old lady who lived nearby lost a cow that somehow strayed across the ravine and became stuck on the other side. The devil saw her plight and offered to build a bridge for her in return for the soul of the first living thing to cross. Having no alternative if she wanted her cow back, the woman accepted his offer and the bridge appeared in front of her. But not to be caught out she threw a biscuit along the span so that a dog ran across, the old lady following safely behind.

Back in town I wasn't surprised to see that the forecast was still predicting a near-gale, so I rang Anna and asked her to change her ticket for Aberystwyth. She was due to arrive just after lunch on Saturday, so in the morning I tidied the boat up, found a birthday card for my father and bought a pair of cheap wrap-around sunglasses that fell apart the next day. Jobs done I strolled around the harbour and along the breakwater, where the waves were crashing against the stonework and sending up clouds of spray. A few anglers sheltered under big umbrellas, but at least it wasn't raining and out of the wind conditions were fairly pleasant. After Anna had arrived and settled herself on board we took a look around Aberystwyth, had a drink in a student-oriented bar, then spent the next hour in a fruitless search for some ginger beer. Admitting defeat we returned to the boat with some more cans of fizzy orange, listened to the forecast, found another Indian restaurant for dinner, and planned our escape.

We awoke early on Sunday to find that the wind had dropped overnight and the morning's forecast was fair with a moderate to fresh southerly, good for crossing Cardigan Bay to Pwllheli. I'd toyed with doing the long haul to Holyhead but Anna wasn't keen and I didn't really want her first passage with me to be a repeat of Phil's Bristol Channel experience. We slipped the berth at 0630, Anna stowed ropes and fenders and I piloted *Indalo* out of the harbour, careful to keep clear of the rocks to the right of the entrance. The sea was still bumpy but having two on board made light work of getting the mainsail up and we were soon passing through the Cynfelin gap, a narrow passage across a submerged causeway of sandbanks, and out into the open sea.

Cardigan Bay is a relatively shallow area of water with several sets of causeways and sandbanks protruding out from the shore like long, groping fingers. Sarn Badrig or Saint Patrick's Causeway (colloquially the Badrigs) is the longest and most significant navigationally, stretching ten miles to seaward. It's traditionally the place where St Patrick walked across to Wales from Ireland, and it's also featured in a story set in the fifth century that's reminiscent of the Cornish legend of Lyonesse. According to tradition the bay was once a land called the Cantre'r Gwaelod, the Lowland Hundred, and Sarn Badrig was part of its sea wall. Being below the level of high water it was defended by a system of dykes, ditches and sluices. A man called Seithennin was responsible for the defences, but he preferred to spend more time drinking and feasting than making his rounds and before long the sea walls fell into disrepair. Eventually the inevitable happened and the sea entered, drowning the sixteen cities of the Cantre'r

Gwaelod and forcing the king, Gwyddno Garanhir, to move his capital to present-day Borth.

There's little doubt that much of the bay was above sea level several thousand years ago, but there was supposedly evidence of drowned settlements close to the coast up until end of the eighteenth century and even now the remains of a submarine forest can be seen near Borth. One theory is that the story of the Cantre'r Gwaelod represents a folk memory stretching back into the remote past, translated when it was written down into a near-contemporary historic account; another is that there were settlements in what's now the bay in historic times, if not on the scale that the story infers. Oceanographers have recently developed techniques to scan the sea bed and map former settlements, so the secrets of Cardigan Bay may soon be revealed.

The rough sea didn't persist much further than Cynfelin so I set a course close to the West Prong, the last area of dangerous shallows at the end of the Badrigs. As we left the Ceredigion coast behind the Llŷn peninsula appeared first as smudges on the horizon, then as a group of islands, and eventually as a continuous coastline backed by steep hills. Finally the island of Bardsey came into view off to the left to complete the picture and as we turned due north towards Pwllheli we made out St Tudwal's Island off Abersoch. The sun came out as *Indalo* cleared the Prong, and a little while later we sighted our first boats of the day: two yachts out of Abersoch, a fishing boat, a fleet of dinghies racing around some inflatable buoys, a crabber inspecting pots, and then maybe a dozen yachts heading in or out of Pwllheli. We spotted the red-and-white buoy that marks the main fairway into the harbour, lowered the sail, and made a careful entrance to tie up in what turned out to be a sizeable, smart and well-equipped (and expensive) marina.

Pwllheli is the chief town of the Llŷn peninsula and it was once an active port, but the harbour has gradually silted up and apart from a few fishing boats it's now mainly a yachting centre. The marina occupies a dredged area of the harbour some way away from the main town, a little like the nautical equivalent of a caravan park. Nevertheless there's something quite attractive about its open, flat aspect in this country of hills. Some sensitive shrub and wildflower planting helps brighten up the marina surroundings while also emphasising their bleakness, as if the plants are making a point of hanging on against the elements. The whole effect is one of uncluttered openness that brings to mind parts of the west of Ireland. Hopefully it will remain that way and not become blighted by the kind of anonymous marina development that's springing up around much of the British coast.

We walked into town around the large, abandoned inner harbour. A tidy block-paved path led to a smart and tasteful but almost deserted promenade that followed the harbour wall around to the railway station and main shopping area. We counted an oystercatcher, a few cormorants and three herons in the harbour, and nothing else other than some driftwood and a couple of shopping trolleys in the mud. I couldn't see any litter and there were no overweight people smoking at the back of the supermarket, though one of the herons was definitely oversized. From what we could see Pwllheli itself seemed fairly self-contained and unremarkable, if a little quiet late on Sunday afternoon. There was a sizeable Spar supermarket that had the provisions we needed for an evening meal, though once again it didn't stock ginger beer. I was beginning to wonder if the Welsh had something against the drink. At least the Mitre was open, one of those pubs that could either be traditional and unspoilt or tarted-up and scruffy. It turned out to be the former, it had some attractive carved woodwork, and it served good enough bar meals to persuade Anna to save the provisions for the next day.

Our task for Monday was to get to Porth Dinllaen on the other side of the Llŷn, a distance of maybe half-a-dozen miles by foot but more than thirty by sea. We had to wait until mid-day to set out because leaving any earlier would have meant running into an adverse tide in Bardsey Sound, at five to six knots strong enough to keep us from getting anywhere. So we had coffee in the marina café, then we went for a stroll around the boatyard and marina precincts where I found a chandlery and bought a Manx flag and a few other bits and pieces. We spent the rest of the morning studying the boats that were still laid up in the yard, then we had another coffee and got ready to depart.

Setting off at half-past twelve we decided to sail in close to Abersoch, keeping inshore of the offlying St Tudwal's islands. The sea was choppy in the harbour mouth and there was something of a breeze, but it soon died away and left the engine to do the work. Abersoch looked beguiling with boats moored in the bay and a varied collection of houses on the beach and climbing up the headland. I promised myself that I'd anchor there on some future voyage, or at least call by in the car. Passing the islands we made good progress through St Tudwal's Roads and down to the cliffs of Trwyn Cilan, the southernmost point of the Llŷn, where we turned westwards for Bardsey. Then we ran into the tide. In truth it was only a couple of knots, but it slowed our progress to the pace of a fast walk. It did though give us time to admire the sweeping cliffs of Braich-y-Pwll on the mainland side and contemplate the mysterious, mist-clad isle of Bardsey, the Island of Twenty Thousand Saints where St David is reputed to be buried, Christians took refuge in the fifth century, and an endless stream of pilgrims made the crossing.

Eventually we began to pull clear of Bardsey and head north-eastwards along this scenic stretch of the Llŷn. Tall cliffs gave way to a gentler coastline with villages strung out behind low bluffs, then successive headlands came into view against a mountainous backdrop. Approaching the headland of Carreg Ddu that shelters Porth Dinllaen from the west we were passed by a big Bénéteau yacht which turned into the bay and sought out a spot to anchor. We followed it in and did likewise, but the wind was strengthening from the north and there was a fair swell coming in. A chance conversation in the marina at Pwllheli had revealed that there was another anchorage about a mile away at Porth Nefyn that was more sheltered in northerlies, so we moved and anchored there a little way from a lifeboat station: still rolling uncomfortably, but with less danger of the anchor dragging. To make doubly sure I ran an old fourteen-pound hammerhead halfway along the anchor chain to help keep it flat on the sea bed.

Today Porth Dinllaen and Porth Nefyn together provide havens for a few fishing boats and leisure craft, but in the nineteenth century they were an important port of call for coasters and hardly a day would go by without a couple of craft calling in to offload some cargo. Porth Dinllaen was almost chosen as the rail terminus and departure port for Dublin, but the committee that was called to decide on the final location voted by a majority of one for Holyhead. From seaward Porth Nefyn itself consists of little more than a few houses straggling along the shore with some others up above on the coast road, but its backdrop of hills and mountains borders on the spectacular.

Anna was determined to use the vegetables she had bought in Pwllheli, so she cooked something up with a can of goulash, some beans, herbs, rice, leeks and broccoli, and I scoured the stores for my last bottle of red wine, a rather excellent Fitou that had somehow managed to survive from last year's trip to Normandy. The meal was appetising and most welcome, though the swell coming in to the anchorage meant that as soon as dinner was finished we washed the dishes and got our heads down. Still bothered about the anchor dragging, I programmed a GPS to alert me if we drifted off anywhere and set my alarm for three-hourly intervals. But by my second call at 0430 the wind had moved around to the south, the swell had gone and we were sitting calmly pointing towards the shore.

Before leaving the Welsh mainland behind there's a tale that doesn't belong directly to any of the places I visited but it's nautical, intriguing, and it has echoes of the St Brendan story I mentioned earlier. It starts in 1169 with the death of Owain Gwynedd ap Gruffydd, king of north Wales and father of nineteen children including the nautically-inclined Madog (or Madoc). Bowing out of the ensuing rivalry for the succession, Madog and his brother Riryd set sail from Abercerrig (Rhos-on-Sea) in two ships, the *Gorn Gwynant* and the *Pedr Sant*. Madog returned two years later with tales of a great land to the west, setting out this time with ten ships, a party of settlers and a herd of cattle. He was never seen again in Wales but he was rumoured to have made a landfall in what is now Mobile Bay, settling on the banks of the Alabama river.

The Madog story was quoted widely in the sixteenth century to bolster Elizabeth I's claim to North America over that of Spain. Books have been written both supporting and disparaging it, and the evidence is persuasive if hardly conclusive. Explorers in the eighteenth century claimed to have met 'white Indians' who spoke a language akin to Welsh, later identified with the Mandan people whose architecture and boats bore a resemblance to mediaeval Welsh designs. Nevertheless the young explorer John Evans who set out specifically to find evidence of Welsh settlement came away empty-handed (apart, so it was rumoured, from some Spanish currency), the Mandans were decimated by smallpox, and the story started to lose credibility. A more recent twist was added when DNA tests were claimed to support the theory that there were Welsh settlers in America going back eight hundred years or more.

By lunchtime the sun had come out and the day was pleasantly warm despite a breeze that promised a passage to Holyhead under sail. We raised the mainsail, weighed anchor and sailed off at half-past two. A moderate to fresh breeze had got up from the west, enough to push *Indalo* along at slightly more than six knots. I set the windvane to take us north and thought we were on for a steady passage to Holy-head, but it wasn't to be and the wind was no more than a sea breeze: half an hour offshore it dropped and our speed nearly halved. We struggled on for another half-hour, determined to cross the 53°N line of latitude under sail. Now with engine on and foresail furled away progress was slow against the tide, but the low-lying Anglesey coastline gradually came into view away to the east, with the higher ground of Holy Island directly ahead. Soon we could pick out faint flashes from South Stack lighthouse and gradually the atmospheric outline of the Stack itself became visible, a rocky islet joined to the cliffs of Holy Island by a narrow bridge at the foot of a steep zigzag path. The current was now in our favour and as we rounded South Stack and altered course for North Stack the sea became choppy. A Wayfarer sailing dinghy played in the white water off North Stack, fighting against the tide. We waved to the lone occupant and he waved back: he seemed to be enjoying himself.

We entered Holyhead harbour shortly before eight in the evening, passed the ferry terminal, and made our way along the side of the breakwater – at 1.87 miles Britain's longest – before tying up to a walk-ashore pontoon. We walked ashore. The marina offices and facilities were in a series of temporary buildings at the end of a building site, but they were closed for the evening. The sailing club was empty and the sea-front promenade almost deserted. According to the chart the main part of the town seemed to be inland a little between the marina and the ferry terminal, so we turned left along the promenade and right into a side street, which took us into a suburb with the odd shop, a pub, and a few eating-places, mostly closed. Eventually we found an Indian restaurant that was still open, Anna's second and my third in a week.

For no particular reason we took a day off on Wednesday. The day was warm and sunny with a gentle breeze. The marina offices were open and after paying our dues we were encouraged to look at a scale model of a development that would include a facilities block, a restaurant, offices, shops and apartments. Improvements to the current arrangements were definitely needed and it would have been good to have somewhere to eat nearby when we came ashore, but from what I could see the design could have been more in tune with the surroundings. The developer selected to for the works was called Pochin. I wondered if the name was pronounced anything like the drink, whether there was any connection given Holyhead's connection with Ireland, and if the development had been designed under its influence.

We thought about climbing up Holyhead Mountain, which is crowned by a prehistoric earthwork and has views to the Lake District, Snowdonia, the Isle of Man, the Mountains of Mourne and County Wicklow. What we actually did was to walk along the promenade again and find the town centre, slightly further on than where we had got to the previous night. Holyhead, Caergybi in Welsh, the resting-place of St Cybi, is a down-to-earth place dominated by its role as the ferry port for Dublin. It's hardly an affluent seaside resort but it's not really any the worse for that. The centre was far from depressed and it seemed the kind of place where there was probably plenty to do if you took time to go and find it. There were a lot of seemingly unemployed men hanging around outside pubs, but the atmosphere was friendly and people (unemployed or busy) took time to say hello and exchange a few words. Ignoring the accents for a moment it was easy to imagine being over in Ireland: the style of the streets and houses, the landscape, and the general demeanour of the place all reflected something that could have come from across the water.

We decided to eat on board so Anna bought some lamb, vegetables and mint sauce to cook up something appropriately Welsh, although – and this was the last chance for Wales to redeem itself – we couldn't find any ginger beer. Back at the harbour there were yachts tacking around the moored boats and dinghies racing around buoys in the evening sun, and a large fast ferry was in port with what looked like 'TRĪSH FERRIES' written on its side. After dinner I rang my father to wish him a happy birthday while Anna spoke to her daughter, who had been unwell. Unfortunately the news wasn't good: she wasn't recovering as expected. Anna didn't want to rush home immediately, but I sensed she was a little anxious and wouldn't be coming with me to Oban as we had hoped. My intended route to the Scottish west coast was based on having two people on board, so unless I could arrange for someone else to join I'd have to rethink. But that could wait for the moment. Tomorrow's job was to get to the Isle of Man.

4

In the sea of Manannan

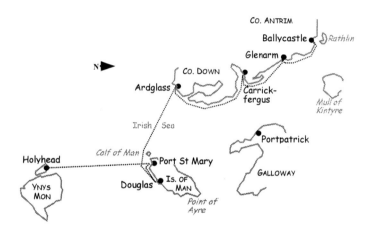

Thursday morning brought forth a miserable dankness under a cold grey sky. We slipped our lines at half-past seven and motored out of the harbour in a flat calm, ghosting past the Skerries rocks at the northern end of Anglesey. I set the autohelm on a course I'd calculated earlier, leaving little for us to do other than keep watch, feel cold, drink tea and visit the heads. Twenty miles out from Holyhead the isle of Anglesey faded out of sight and we were on our own in a grey sea under a lighter grey sky. It was nearly noon, but it felt as if we were still waiting for dawn to break. The monotony was broken by two dolphins surfacing in the distance, then a fender came undone from the stern rail and bobbed in our wake, making us practice our man overboard drill. Not long afterwards a cargo ship crossed half a mile in front of us on its way from Liverpool to Dublin, followed by another one going in the opposite direction. A little later the Isle of Man took shape as an indistinct smudge of grey between the grey of the sea and the grey of the sky. As the passage drew to a close the dankness began to disperse and the wind picked up enough for us to sail the last few miles into Port St Mary. We turned into the welcoming little harbour, paused on a mooring buoy for a cup of tea, then once we'd got our bearings we moved over to the quay and rafted up against a big yacht that was bound for Dublin early next morning.

I'd never been to the Isle of Man before. When I was a child we had half-considered a holiday there, so I'd seen the brochures and remembered that Douglas was the capital and there was a big waterfall somewhere and a water wheel somewhere else, maybe Laxey. I knew the island had its own government like Jersey and Guernsey and they still used the birch on offenders (or they might have stopped by now following pressure from the European Union or Amnesty International or somebody). I once went on a date with a Manx girl but I can only remember her saying the island was a bit parochial and that they had only just been dragged into the twentieth century (and that was in the mid-nineties). Oh, and Manx cats are tailless and the Manx emblem is a star made up of three legs because Manxmen are good at legging it. I needed to find out a bit more.

Ellan Vannin, the Isle of Man, has a population of about seventy-five thousand of which a third live in Douglas. The island has been ruled from Norway, Scotland and England, though it's had its own parliament called the Tynwald since 979, claimed to be the oldest continuous parliament in the world (Iceland's is older but it was suspended for forty-five years). Today it's a British dependency subject to the Queen as Lord of Mann, but it isn't part of England, the United Kingdom or the European Union. There are no customs formalities for visiting yachts as there are in the Channel Islands, though as we were to find out there is a Manx customs service. The island is an offshore financial centre and tax haven, this and tourism having displaced the traditional industries of farming and fishing as the main income-earners; there's a growing high-tech manufacturing sector too, which the Douglas government is keen to encourage. The island's heritage is a mix of Norse, Celtic and English and it has its own language which is used in official titles but isn't widely spoken. And the three-legged symbol is called a triskelion and goes with the island's motto of *quocunque ieceris stabit,* 'wherever it's thrown, it will stand.' Maybe Manx people tend to land on their feet.

After I'd hoisted my triskelion flag in place of the Welsh dragon we set out to explore Port St Mary. A road took us a short distance along the coast, then we followed a path back around a golf course and into the village. A raised walkway ran from the centre along the coast in the direction of the harbour, and it would have made for a pleasant stroll back except that the tide was out revealing an unpleasant smell of seaweed and sewage. Other than that the village was attractive enough with a mixture of picturesque cottages, suburban bungalows and a rather stylish renovated apartment block. There seemed to be more art and craft shops than places to buy basic provisions, though we managed to pick up the few things we needed and find a very acceptable pub-restaurant on the way back.

Back aboard the weather forecast was for a gentle to fresh northerly on Friday, increasing to a near-gale over the weekend. My plan for the next passage had been to anchor at Peel on the north-western coast of the island before heading north to Portpatrick in Scotland. I was looking forward to calling in at Peel and visiting its nautical museum, the House of Manannan: Manannan is the Celtic sea-god who in times of threat is said to wreath the island named after him in mist. But the harbour is exposed to the north, so it wouldn't do to be caught there in a strong northerly. I discussed some of the other options with Anna, and eventually we settled on Douglas because its inner harbour is completely sheltered and, should the weather keep us there, it's the hub for the island's bus service.

We set out in the morning under an overcast sky, soon clearing to bright sun and a gentle but cool easterly breeze. There was no hurry so we set full sail and tacked slowly up the coast, the windvane holding each course. Just over half-way our attention was attracted by two motorboats heading towards us from the direction of Douglas. I worked out they should just clear us astern when the smaller one, a rigid inflatable, peeled off and with a deft manoeuvre dropped in just behind *Indalo's* rudder and slowed to our speed. The two young women on board indicated they wanted to talk to us so I motioned them to come alongside. They turned out to be Manx customs officers and they took us through a questionnaire to establish who we were and where we were from. I offered to heave to and let them come aboard to rummage in my lockers, but they declined.

Two tacks later we were heading into Douglas and rapidly removing items of clothing as the full force of the midday sun made itself felt in the shelter of the harbour. The yacht berths are on the other side of a swing bridge that lifts up every hour, and we had a short wait before it swung and we were let in. The marina attendant directed us to tie up to the quay close to a packed pub, convenient enough but with the risk of beer cans and inebriated patrons dropping in. I'd completely forgotten was that it was the last day of TT week, the island's celebrated motorcycle races, so we couldn't have arrived at a busier time even if we'd visited on August bank holiday.

When I came back from the harbour office Anna had spoken to her daughter and she was beginning to think about getting back. My original plan was that we would go to Portpatrick, work our way up through the Firth of Clyde, take the Crinan Canal through to the west coast, and part company at Oban. Without crew the canal is really a non-starter, so I would need to take the seaward route around the Mull of Kintyre. The forecast had improved slightly for Saturday, but the wind was still due to be a fresh northerly. Added to that the timing of the tides would make it difficult to get from Douglas to Portpatrick in one go, and with the wind on the nose it would be a long and unpleasant passage with little chance of arriving before nightfall. I pored over my chart of the Irish Sea: maybe we could make for somewhere on the south coast of Galloway? It still meant beating or motoring into the wind, and Anna wouldn't have an easy journey home even if we could get to Portpatrick the following day. I sat racking my brains and checking tides and bus links, but nothing worked so I gave up.

Next time I looked at the chart the answer was obvious: Anna could fly from Belfast, and I could follow the Irish coast north. We could make an early start, leave Douglas on the last bridge swing of the morning, backtrack past Port St Mary, cross the Irish Sea westwards with the wind nicely on the beam, and drop into Ardglass in County Down. If Sunday was fine we could continue on to Belfast Lough, otherwise my almanac said there was a bus to Belfast via Portpatrick. Anna said she would think about it but I'd already pictured *Indalo* making a landfall in Ardglass and as we went ashore I had the Blondie tune *Heart of Glass* playing in my head.

Douglas was both bigger than I'd expected from the little I had already seen of it, and more of a seaside resort and shopping centre than I'd imagined. It had some fine old buildings including the market house, a rather grand seaside terrace, and some tall houses overlooking the harbour. Up by the sea front a big screen showing highlights of the TT races was being watched by a large crowd of assorted bikers and holidaymakers. We weren't in Douglas long enough to get a real impression of the place, though for me it didn't have the same instant appeal or mix of the familiar and the foreign that

I'd felt when I first visited St Helier or St Peter Port. To be fair I might have had a different opinion if I'd come at a quieter time. Most of the seaward-facing eateries were packed out, but eventually we found a quiet café in an attractive galleried shopping centre where we were the only customers other than a whole shift of local police. They had piped music from the seventies and eighties playing in the background, including of course *Heart of Glass*. So Ardglass it was.

Saturday 11th June, day 29, started with an 0330 awakening. It seemed premature to be leaving the Isle of Man so soon but the weather was promising and I was looking forward to arriving in Ireland. We were soon motoring carefully past the swing bridge and through the outer harbour of a yet-to-awaken Douglas, with the promise of a gentle or moderate northerly to help us on our way. Port St Mary went past in two hours, half the time it had taken to sail in the opposite direction on Friday, and half an hour later we were clearing the Calf of Man and once more entering the open waters of the Irish Sea. The wind was northwesterly, now no more than a gentle breeze, but it was enough to raise the waves into a confused wind-against-tide chop. Less than an hour out from the Calf *Indalo*'s speed dropped to four knots and our slow pace became uncomfortable in the rolling sea. I started the engine and set the autopilot, then retired below for a short break while Anna kept watch. When I came back on deck the Isle of Man had disappeared and the Irish coast had yet to show on the horizon, but the sea was now much flatter and more comfortable. Unusually for British or Irish waters this part of the Irish Sea is almost completely free of tidal currents, so for the moment I could steer directly for Ardglass without worrying about being swept downstream of my destination.

When Anna reappeared we could make out the Mountains of Mourne in the distance, but as yet the relatively low-lying coast of County Down hadn't come into focus. It took shape gradually, and five miles offshore we could pick out what looked like Ardglass. The GPS confirmed our impressions and we dropped the mainsail and headed through the narrow entrance into the rock-strewn harbour. The main port inside the brakwater is home to the fishing fleet, but just beyond is another little bay called Phennick Cove where there's a small marina. There were plenty of unoccupied pontoons available so we tied up to one, boiled the kettle and reported to the marina office.

I felt pleased to be in Ireland and, though I'd never visited Ardglass before I somehow felt that I was on familiar ground. I'd been to various parts of the island over the last fifteen years, often working my way up the west coast from Kerry, Clare or Galway to Derry and Antrim, and I have many happy memories of both north and south. My overriding impression is of a relatively relaxed and friendly land, and that includes the northern province: even back in the early nineties my strongest impressions were less of the problems and dangers of the 'Troubles' and more of the helpful and talkative nature of the people I met. Anna's memories were less positive, but I was confident that this time she would come away with a different view.

Ardglass (Green Hill) was founded by Anglo-Norman settlers in the twelfth century and it has no less than seven castles or tower houses, built mainly to defend the incomers against the locals. Its harbour is far older and it was used as a natural refuge three thousand years ago, continuing to grow and prosper up until its heyday in the mid-nineteenth century when four or five hundred fishing boats would crowd in with their catches of herring. Even now there is a fair-sized fishing fleet and an active processing and marketing industry based on the quay. By contrast the marina, and even the bay that it is in, is much more recent. Phennick Cove in its natural form was a shallow, rocky inlet able to accommodate only the smallest boats. Ten years ago a mix of local initiative and national and European support led to the rock being carved out, the cove deepened and a harbour constructed that's able to take all but the very largest yachts. The result is an attractive haven with good facilities in a low-key but unusual building, the whole thing fitting the scale and ambience of Ardglass itself. It's also very well-run by a locally managed not-for-profit company, and the welcome I received was typical of what I was to experience over the next few weeks throughout Ireland and Scotland.

After catching up on some sleep we took a walk along the coast and through the village, stumbled on the Old Commercial bar, and had a glass of Guinness each. The Old Commercial is one of those unmistakeably Irish pubs with the locals seemingly resident at the bar and a fine collection of bottles and polished barrels behind it. Finishing my glass I donated two pocketfuls of accumulated coppers to the model lifeboat and we wandered off to look for somewhere to eat. The first place we considered was Aldo's, a converted three-storey terraced town house with a relaxed ambience and a good menu, but we dragged ourselves away and opted for the marina manager's recommendation, the golf club. The clubhouse is probably the grandest of Ardglass's castles or tower houses and it's claimed to be the oldest clubhouse in the world. It was homely rather than plush inside, but the food was good as were the views.

The next day the weather forecast was for a fresh to strong northwesterly breeze, so rather than getting cold and wet flogging up to Belfast Lough we decided to stay put and explore. Ardglass is an unpretentious and down-to-earth yet attractive town or village, and with the excellent marina it was a good find and a fortunate ill wind that brought us across the Irish Sea. It hasn't escaped violence and vandalism but it's never been at the centre of the troubles and it doesn't seem particularly scarred by them. It's difficult to work out where the town centre is unless it's the harbour itself, as the shops, bars and eating-places (and the castles) are spread around various streets, not always in the most obvious spots. Apart from the golf club I found a castle that's now an elderly people's home and another smaller but more castle-like one called Jordan's Castle that's still a castle, at least in the sense that it isn't used for anything else. In fact it was the only one of the seven to see action, having been besieged at the end of the sixteenth century before being relieved from the sea. The whereabouts of the other four I never found out.

Taking a walk out of Ardglass I encountered typical lowland Irish country with bungalows, more bungalows, lush green fields, derelict bungalows with big gardens, semi-wild hedgerows, and more lush green fields with the odd bungalow. Even the modern bungalows have something about them that is unmistakeably Irish, and compared with England and Wales (and much of lowland Scotland for that matter) there's a feeling of having space to play with. On the way back I took a diversion along the northern edge of the harbour on a rough path over rocks and between clumps of grass. It provided good views of the marina, the fishing harbour and the village, along with old batteries, clothes, tyres, plastic fish cartons, a rusty wing off a car and a couple of hundred pink rubber gloves, size small. Ardglass might be an attractive place in general but it has the most litter-strewn beach I've ever seen, and I hardly think that lot was washed up from a shipwreck.

Back on board the forecast for Monday was ideal, a moderate to fresh southwesterly. Making use of the tide we could leave at lunchtime and get to Bangor or Carrickfergus before nightfall, then Anna could leave the next morning for Belfast and home. What actually happened was that the wind veered and we were faced with a near-gale from the north-west, so we stayed put. There wouldn't be enough time the next day to get to Belfast Lough and for Anna to get home, so she chose to catch the bus and fly a day early.

I accompanied Anna as far as Downpatrick where there's a connecting bus to Belfast. Our first bus took a roundabout route out of Ardglass but it did let us see Killough, a village with a straight, wide tree-lined main street, another feature that seems to appear far more this side of the Irish Sea than it does back home. We arrived at Downpatrick in light rain and Anna boarded her onward bus while I walked off in the direction of the town centre, which was pleasant enough but hardly exciting in the drizzle. Its best feature was a fascinating hardware store that stocked all sorts of oddments that the owner brought out in little cardboard boxes. I wanted some small brass hinges for a locker door that had just come unhinged: they were so cheap I bought two pairs in different sizes, just in case.

Downpatrick is County Down's county town, and it's also the earthly resting-place of Saint Patrick. I picked up a map at the tourist office behind the bus station, and decided to visit the cathedral and the town museum before returning to the town's St Patrick Centre. The museum, housed in an old prison, was closed for renovation. The cathedral seemed closed to visitors too, though the woman at the desk in the St Patrick Centre told me that I could probably have gone in quietly at the back while the service was going on. She also told me there was no need to pay to visit the Centre unless I wanted to see the exhibition, so I just had a look at some static displays and browsed the shelves in the bookshop. I hadn't realised that the 'exhibition' was actually the main display so I came away without finding out very much about St Patrick, though I did find a copy of Tim Severin's book on the Brendan voyage and started reading it over a cup of tea while I was waiting for the bus.

Arriving back in Ardglass I thought I'd visit Jordan's Castle but like half of Downpatrick it was closed, or maybe I just hadn't worked out that I was supposed to scale the battlements or get in through a culvert. So I went to the boat and put the hinges on my locker, entered some waypoints in the GPS and checked the weather again. The forecast was for the wind to turn back to a southwesterly and drop to gentle or moderate, which would give me a good run up to Belfast Lough. Because the time of high water had advanced by nearly another hour I brought my departure time forward to early morning , allowing me to leave the familiar port in half-light and enter the unfamiliar one in full daylight rather than the other way around. I prepared everything for the passage then went off to find some food before getting an early night. Resisting the temptation to have a three-course meal at Aldo's I settled for the fish-and-chip café, ordering a fresh and tasty cod and falling in with the crew of a steel yacht called *Kalima*, bound southwards for Cornwall and France.

I turned in at nine o'clock in the hope of getting a few hours sleep, but just as I was setting my mobile phone alarm my father rang at what to him was a reasonable hour to see how I was doing: I'd been going a month now, he reminded me. According to my grand plan I should have been in Portpatrick yesterday and moving on to the Clyde tomorrow, the equivalents on the Irish side being Belfast Lough and Glenarm, so I was two days behind schedule. On the other hand I'd lost at least a week and a half to gales and strong winds, so I couldn't complain too much. I was already 570 miles from home, over a quarter of the way around, and I had crossed the Bristol Channel and Irish Sea and sailed in waters new to me and probably to *Indalo*. Nevertheless the weather was still unseasonal and there had only been three or four really warm and sunny days so far. It was sure to improve, I told myself, and the best bit in terms of coastline, exploration and pure sense of satisfaction was just beginning. I switched the phone off and went to sleep.

My alarm went off at two and momentarily I had to think where I was, what day it was, and what I was meant to be doing. I was in Ardglass, it was the fourteenth of June, and I was setting out for Belfast Lough. There wasn't a breath of wind in the rigging or a ripple on the water's surface, and the first glimmerings of dawn could be made out in the sky. By the time I slipped my lines it was light enough to see any hazards in the water, or it would have been if not for the blinding floodlight that illuminated the fish quay. Several fishing boats were also leaving harbour so I made my way out with them. It was good to be out early and setting off on a decent-length single-handed passage again. Outside the harbour there was a faint breeze from the south-west, so I hoisted the mainsail in case it strengthened. The sky was heavily overcast, although according to yesterday's forecast rain wasn't expected; but nor was a lack of wind. I set a course to take me past Strangford Lough, and the rain set in.

Strangford Lough is a superb natural harbour about fifteen miles long by three or four wide, on the chart making a shape that looks like a leaping salmon. The long entrance channel to the salmon's tail is subject to fierce tides and the upper part is littered with rocks and shallows, but the lough is claimed to be well worth the careful navigation that's needed. I'd thought about stopping off there, but it's only a short hop from Ardglass, the tides mean it's not ideal as a passage port, and it's really a small cruising ground in itself that would need a spare day or two to do it justice. I gazed towards the entrance: like Abersoch and Peel, another place to come back to when I get time.

My next waypoint was the South Rock light buoy, more like a miniature lightship rather than a standard red navigational buoy. From there I tracked around the relatively flat coast of the Ards peninsula, keeping a respectable distance off to avoid the rocks and reefs. Portavogie went by, then Ballywater with its offlying reefs, Millisle, Templepatrick, and finally Donaghadee, the last three merging into one another. The entrance to Donaghadee was signposted on the harbour wall and looked tempting, but with the tide falling and without a detailed chart the chances were that I would run aground in the entrance. So I carried on for

Donaghadee Sound, a passage inside a small island that cuts about five miles and some potentially rough water off the southern entrance to Belfast Lough. From seaward it looked quite wide, but according to the chart the area is full of hidden dangers and the only safe channel is a narrow stretch of water marked by red and green buoys. The channel was easy enough to see, and knowing that the tide could sweep *Indalo* off course and on to the rocks I sighted up on the furthest buoy with a hand-compass to keep me from straying.

Now in Belfast Lough I set a diagonal course for Carrick-fergus, which sits on the north bank a few miles upstream. If the lough had been busy I should have crossed over directly to the north side before following the coast in, but I couldn't see any ships entering or leaving. I noted what I thought was a shore installation, a curious-looking object with three pairs of tall columns like chimneys, but after a few moments I realised it was a gas or oil service vessel heading outwards on the Carrickfergus side. Ship safely past I dropped the mainsail and tied it down, then as if on cue the wind, which had never been more than a light breeze on the whole passage, veered westerly and got up its strength. I was cold and slightly damp and with less than five miles to go I didn't feel like hoisting the sail again, so I just smiled at the perversity of the weather, called up the marina, and put the ropes and fenders out ready to go in.

Carrickfergus marina is a fairly large modern affair surrounded by smart if rather soulless marina development blocks. It's in its own harbour, not even sharing an entrance with the fishing quay. Once moored I tried to orient myself among the maze of pontoons and eventually worked out how to get to the harbour office and facilities. I signed in, received a hefty pack promoting the borough of Carrickfergus, then had a shower in the excellent facility block to warm up. At the opposite end of the marina there's a pub-restaurant called the Windrose, so I went in for a snack and a pint of Guinness. After catching up on some sleep I set off to explore the town and find a proper meal. It was still drizzling and Carrick-fergus seemed drab and uninteresting and I couldn't find anywhere I liked the look of, so I wandered back to the Windrose for another pint of Guinness and a main course to follow the prawn cocktail I'd had earlier.

Getting back into the marina involves pressing a button and speaking on an intercom to the receptionist, who looks out of the window, works out that I'm not a terrorist or a yacht rustler, and releases the gate. There's another intercom to get into the compound that contains the bins and the toilet and shower block and yet another to get into the block itself. It was slightly disconcerting at first, like being in a high-security facility. Press button: "Visitor – *Indalo*." "Opening" (click). Press next button, wait for the voice asking me to identify myself. "Go ahead" (click). They're awake, I thought. Five minutes later back at the gate, press button, "Visitor – *Indalo*." No response. Maybe they wanted a password. Let's guess: it's the fourteenth of June so try "King Billy." I hope this doesn't happen between leaving the marina and wanting to get into the toilet block. "Sorry – go ahead" (click). I'm in.

Reading my Borough of Carrickfergus pack later in the day I realised that I'd just missed the annual pageant and re-enactment of the landing of William of Orange. William arrived on 14th June 1690 to begin his campaign against the recently-deposed James II. Calculating that he would get most support against the Protestant William in Ireland because of its majority Catholic population, James had landed in Dublin in March of the previous year. He quickly took control of the country except for Derry and Enniskillen, which he besieged. By the time William stepped off his ship his army had already lifted the sieges and regained much of the north, but despite an early victory at the celebrated (or notorious, depending which side you're on) Battle of the Boyne it took his forces more than a year to drive the Jacobite supporters out of Ireland. King Billy is still revered by Ulster

Protestants, but James, who fled to France soon after things started going against him, was regarded as selling out on his Catholic supporters and earned himself the unfortunate nickname of Séamus á Chaca. I won't translate.

Among the places of interest on the map in my pack I noticed that in addition to the very conspicuous castle on the other side of the main harbour the town had a gasworks museum. I wasn't sure that poking around a gasworks was the best thing to be doing on a Wednesday morning, but I read on and apparently it was the last gasworks in Ireland where gas was extracted from coal, a process that went on until the late 1960s and presumably the arrival of natural gas from the North Sea. Town gas it was called when I was a lad, and I'm sure we were a few years behind Ireland because I can remember our fires being converted to take the new stuff in the early seventies. I decided to go and have a look. The entrance was in a back street and it looked just like a shop, but unfortunately it was closed until after lunch. I wasn't having much luck with museums lately so I visited the castle instead.

Carrickfergus Castle is one of the most conspicuous bastions of English rule in Ireland. The keep is Norman, dating from 1178, with subsequent additions up to Elizabethan times. It saw action across several centuries up until 1760 when it was defended against the French, then it was garrisoned in the Napoleonic wars and again in the Second World War. As I arrived two school parties had just beaten me to the ticket office, but I escaped them by bounding to the top of the keep and starting my tour from there. There was no access to the roof, but as far as the drizzle permitted there were some worthwhile views up and down the coast out of the windows. In addition to the schoolchildren the castle was full of life-sized figures from different eras in its history, with some Norman soldiers armed with crossbows on the western parapet opposite some of their eighteenth-century counterparts loading a cannon pointing out to the east. There was a figure of the Constable from the fourteenth century, but the one that intrigued me most was Con O'Neill frozen in the act of making his escape in 1603. Con was a prominent local chief with his own castle in Castlereagh and extensive lands at Clandeboye. Some of his men killed some English soldiers in a fight over a consignment of wine, and Con was locked up for abetting them. His escape seems to have been aided by his newly-wed wife and by one Hugh Montgomery, who helped him reach Ayrshire in return for a substantial portion of his lands which rather ironically were then settled by Scots from the area Con had fled to.

Having found a source of ginger beer in Carrickfergus and returned to *Indalo* laden with six-packs, I prepared to set off for my next stop, the little port of Glenarm, mid-afternoon. I motored out of the harbour at four o'clock, hauled the sails up and goosewinged down Belfast Lough with a moderate breeze behind me, steering carefully to keep both sails filled with wind. Hardly an hour passed before the wind dropped enough to call the engine into play. Thirty minutes later I was passing the gas terminal that marks the end of the lough when the wind returned, this time from the northeast. I unfurled the foresail again and set the windvane to steer. The wind brought a cold mizzle and soon the headland at the mouth of the loch, easily visible twenty minutes ago, all but disappeared from view. A ferry loomed out of the mist ahead of me: it was difficult to see what course it was on. I tacked in what I thought was the right direction and it came closer, so I tacked again and put the engine on in case I needed some extra speed. This time I was clear, but the wind must have noticed my lack of faith because it soon deserted me again.

Belfast Lough marks the boundary between County Down to the south and County Antrim to the north, and with it a noticeable change in the landscape. North of the lough the coast presents a series of rolling hills that consolidate into the sheer cliffs of Island Magee, a crescent of land almost cut off from the rest of Antrim by Larne Lough. Heading northwards I kept in the shadow of the cliffs until I passed the Isle of

Muck at the end of the peninsula. I identified the offshore East Maiden lighthouse and its companion Russells Rock, and further off made out the Mull of Kintyre over in Scotland, an indistinct blur on the horizon. Before long I was looking into the mouth of the lough and into Larne itself, where two ferries were waiting at their berths and another was making its way out. I gave way to the emerging ship and set a course to clear an offshore rock before closing with the coast at the dramatic, brooding Ballygally Head, where I caught sight of the long and twisting Antrim coast road. The next headland, McAuley, was the last one before Glenarm. I spotted a yellow buoy marking the end of a pipeline and followed the coastline around, until in front of me there appeared a village marked out by a disused stone mill to port and a church spire in the centre. I dropped the mainsail, headed for the mill, and came into a surprisingly roomy harbour.

Glenarm is one of the delights of the Antrim coast. The harbour dates from the fifteenth century when it was used by fishermen and by monks for trade; it also became an important centre for exporting lime, hence the stone mill. Nowadays it's primarily a marina with modern-style pontoons protected by the original harbour walls and some more recent additions that do a good job of keeping out the swell from heavy seas. As I rounded the breakwater I was hailed by harbourmaster Tom McKnight, who pointed me into a berth. Tom explained the history of the harbour, pointed out the rudimentary shower block, and explained how he saw the place developing in the future. Like Ardglass the idea was for any development to be of a style and scale in keeping with the village, and the new facility block and restaurant that was planned would be in a restored warehouse or barn. There had already been some opposition to the marina and the local people were keeping a watchful eye on further developments, so the sort of anonymous harbourside blocks I had seen at Carrickfergus wouldn't be appearing here.

It was already well into the evening when I got into Glenarm, and by the time I'd tied up the boat and finished talking to Tom it was ten o'clock and too late to do any proper exploring. Catching the tide north would mean leaving at 0600, so I did little more than take a few pictures, have a snack, and turn in. Glenarm deserved better, but maybe not a full day when the forecast was suitable for moving on.

At the appointed hour I set off for my third wet passage in a row. Leaving the harbour behind I kept clear of some shellfish farms, crossed the double bay of Glenarm and Carnlough and headed for the looming bulk of Garron Point where a few houses were hanging on the steep sides of the hill. Next was wide Glenariff bay backed by the village of Cushendall, then continuing the Antrim pattern of glen, head and glen I rounded a less prominent headland that gave way to Glen Dun and its village of Cushendun. This I'd visited from the landward side perhaps ten or twelve years back. It's a preserved National Trust village busy with visitors in season and it was partly laid out in the 1920s by Clough Williams-Ellis, more famous as the architect of Portmeirion in North Wales. *Indalo* was plodding away under motor and autohelm so I readied my camera to take some photographs. Almost on cue the engine began to struggle and lose power. I backed off the throttle, changed into neutral, and gradually increased the revs. No problem there, so there must be something around the propeller. I ran the engine gently in astern and a big clump of seaweed floated to the surface. Changing to ahead *Indalo* seemed to struggle slightly, so I guessed there was still some weed on the prop and settled for a gentle pace of four knots through the water.

At Cushendun I was already making an extra knot over the ground from the tide, and as Glen Dun gave way to the tall cliffs of Runabay Head the stream doubled its strength. From now on the coastline was all steep slopes and high cliffs, no bays or glens for relief. It was surprisingly green:

there were exposed rock faces here and there, but most of even the steepest slopes were verdant and some were wooded. The protruding Torr Head was a stony exception and beyond that Fair Head came into view, its cliffs stacked on top of rocky slopes like a rack of organ pipes. The tide was in full flow now, first three knots, then three and a half: hardly enough time to admire Fair Head before I was past it and shaping a course between the mainland and Rathlin, the island where Robert the Bruce hid out in a cave and learned patience from watching a spider spinning its web. Coming in to Ballycastle I rang the marina, put my ropes and fenders out, and turned gently into a berth. It was still only half-past nine in the morning.

My last visit to Ballycastle had been the summer before I bought *Indalo,* accompanied by a young lady who I was trying without a great deal of success to interest in the boats in the marina. The weather was fair then: today it was grey and miserable. My first priorities were to change my clothes, hang up all the wet gear, have a shower, get some shopping and find some fuel. The shower was in a house that also contained the harbour office, so I could pay my dues at the same time and enquire about the fuel pontoon which I'd failed to spot on the way in. Not due to arrive for another couple of weeks, was the reply: I'd need to go up into the town to the nearest garage. I'd explore first and take my jerry cans up later.

Ballycastle divides more or less into two parts. Along the front it has the character of a small and fairly sedate seaside resort, with a few shops and pubs at the marina end, the Marine Hotel in the middle, and the bowling green, tennis courts, beach and tourist office on the Fair Head side. From the hotel a road runs at a right angle to the beach uphill through a residential area and into the town centre, nearly a mile from the coast. I found the tourist office and picked up a map and some bus timetables, drank coffee in the hotel, then walked up into the centre. The sea front was drab in the drizzle but the main street was attractive enough and in front of the church it opened out into a neat little triangle called, for some reason, The Diamond. It's even a triangle on the map. Eventually I came to a petrol station on the far side of the town centre. It not only had the cheaper red diesel for boats and tractors but, if I brought my cans up, they would run me and the fuel back to the boat. Typical local helpfulness, *and* they wouldn't take any extra money for it.

Now for a moan about the weather. After all the walking and hauling I had another set of wet waterproofs as well as some uncomfortably humid undergarments, and by the time I'd changed out of them the cabin had so much apparel hung and draped around it that it was beginning to look like a laundry room. I was enjoying being in Northern Ireland but I wasn't enjoying the climate. This was the fourth day of rain or drizzle and the temperature seemed well below what it should be in mid-June. Even with five or six layers of clothing on I was feeling chilly at sea, and at night I was still sleeping with my three-seasons sleeping-bag zipped up and the forecabin hatch shut, with only a slight opening in the mainhatch for ventilation. The boat had the atmosphere of dampness and condensation that I'd expect if I was sailing in April or November, and I was seriously considering buying a warm air heater to plug into the marina's electrical supply. I looked at my log and saw that I'd covered 659 nautical miles since leaving Dartmouth. If I'd headed south rather than north I could have been enjoying the sun and warmth in Porto or Figueira da Foz by now.

Not wanting to walk back into town in the rain I donned yet another set of waterproofs and headed for the Marine Hotel. The food was acceptable but not quite up to what I'd expected, and the Guinness was too cold and not as smooth as it had been in Ardglass. It's all the same stuff brewed at St

James's Gate in Dublin, but I'm convinced that they put something in it that's compass-sensitive so that it doesn't travel as well north or east as it does south and west, and the northerners and the Brits have to go to Dublin if they want a decent pint. Last time I was in the southern capital it was so smooth and creamy that it was possible to drink embarrassing amounts without noticing. It was nearly as good in Galway, too. But take it across to London and it catches a chill and tastes bitter by the end of the first glass.

It was still drizzling in the morning, but at least the weather was brighter and warmer with a rising barometer and hope of a better day to come. Before doing anything else I needed to clear the propeller of the seaweed it had collected off Cushendun, which meant either going for a swim or inflating the dinghy. I chose the dinghy, as apart from my reluctance to take a dip in the chilly sea it hadn't been used since Solva and the outboard motor needed a run. So I motored around the harbour for five or ten minutes, took the engine off, then half-deflated one of the tubes so I could grope around under *Indalo*'s hull, clearing the weed with no more inconvenience than a wet arm and ear.

Now the weather was improving I thought I'd go for a short excursion somewhere. My first choice would have been Rathlin, but I'd missed the morning ferry and I didn't want to vacate my berth so I settled for a bus trip to Bushmills. Bushmills is an attractive settlement in its own right but it also has a distillery that goes back to the beginning of the seventeenth century, claimed to be the first anywhere to be granted a licence. Understandably it makes great play of this along with the fact that its whiskey is triple distilled, unlike the average Scotch which only gets two goes (though the Scots will argue that if you're using modern equipment and techniques two are quite enough). I'd done the distillery tour a few years back so I just elected to watch the video and look around the exhibition and the shop. I couldn't resist adding a bottle of Bushmills Malt to the stores: I had one a few years back and it was delicious, a fine smooth taste with a hint of brandy. Since my last visit Bushmills had become more slick and commercialised, and the entrance favours visitors in cars over those on foot. Nevertheless the produce is just as good. In years gone by there used to be a Rathlin ferryman who would open a bottle of the stuff, throw the cork in the sea and invite his favourite passengers to help him finish it off.

Back on board I put my damp gear out in the sun then I rang Rosemary, a friend from Londonderry who I'd unsuccessfully tried to contact when I was in Ardglass. Ballycastle was further from Londonderry than I'd imagined and it was a bit late for her to come over for the evening, and she was busy on Saturday too. I wanted to be in Islay by Sunday at the latest, so we had to leave it at that. A pity as she would have given me an excuse to do a day trip over to Rathlin. So I finished off the navigation to Port Ellen on Islay and did my routine engine checks. Normally these are no more than a formality but this time the gearbox oil was nearly off the dipstick, maybe something to do with the prop getting fouled and making the gearbox overheat. It needed automatic transmission fluid, which I didn't have; though I could probably hold out until Port Ellen. The forecast was for a gentle to fresh south to southeasterly, warm but with a possibility of drizzle, so there was just a chance that the engine would only be needed for a few minutes at either end.

Jobs done, I put my slightly less damp gear back below, then went for a walk to see Ballycastle in sunlight. I ambled along the beach, took some photographs of the town and of Fair Head, then crossed a little footbridge to take a country route back into the town centre. It was a fair puff up Dun-a-Mallaght Road but good exercise for the legs and lungs, and I was rewarded with views across to Rathlin, Fair Head and in the distance the Mull of Kintyre. No sign of Islay though: the northern horizon was obscured by haze. I followed a track across a valley and back into town, where I picked on the Cellar Restaurant for dinner purely because it was in the Triangle (sorry, Diamond) and below ground. It was intimate and cosy with tables set between pews, and the food was up to the mark too. It was a good farewell to Ballycastle and to Ireland, though it would have been good to have some company to share it with.

5

Through the Great Gate

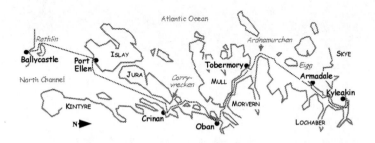

It was Saturday the 18th of June, day 36, and the middle third of my voyage, the Scottish leg, was about to begin. In mist and a gentle breeze I left Ballycastle harbour at a quarter past seven and motored across Rathlin Sound to Bull Point, the western tip of Rathlin and at 6°18'.1 W what was to be the westernmost point of my voyage. The wind picked up to a fresh breeze from the northeast, dropped momentarily, then once I was clear of the island it returned with slightly less force from just south of east. I set a course under full sail and let the windvane do the steering while I kept a careful watch in the mist: visibility was a couple of miles at most and there's a shipping lane between Rathlin and Islay. As it turned out I saw or heard no ships and I was alone in my circle of sea for most of the way across. Eventually another yacht appeared through the mist heading in the same direction, followed by a fishing boat and then a second yacht from the east. Still no sign of Islay, but we were all converging on an invisible green buoy a mile and a half away. Some distance ahead a ship, probably the Port Ellen car ferry, appeared from the north-east and turned in just as the island started to take shape. I spotted the green buoy, sailed into the wide bay of Port Ellen and dropped the sails before motoring under the nose of the now-moored ferry to a pontoon berth close to the village. I tied up, packed up and at noon I stepped ashore.

Port Ellen must be one of the strangest ports on the whole of the British coast, though I don't mean that to be a criticism. The harbour itself is rather charming: a natural bay fringed with rocks and sand and backed by once-grand houses and hotels on the quayside, thinning to a characteristically Scottish village terrace, then thinning again to individual houses and bungalows on the wilder northern shore. There's a feel about it that brings to mind a more austere version of Hugh Town in the Isles of Scilly, but it also has the uniformity and unrealness of a planned settlement. The effect is slightly marred by an ugly ferry terminal with 'PORT ELLEN' in big industrial-unit letters on the side of a big and depressing-looking industrial unit. Ashore the village is both seductive and sad. Seductive because of its self-sufficient feel, Tardis-like shops crammed with all the necessities for living in a remote Scottish village, friendly people, down-to-earth cottages and make-your-own-entertainment attitude. Sad because of the number of derelict or boarded-up houses, including one that was once a fairly smart hotel. I might have expected to find somewhere like this far out in the western isles, but hardly as my first stop in Scotland on the southern-most of the Inner Hebrides.

There isn't that much for the casual visitor to do in Port Ellen other than explore the village, buy supplies, have a shower, use the bar, and walk out into the surrounding countryside where it's almost impossible not to encounter a distillery (there are three in as many miles in one direction and a disused one in the other). I put off a longer walk or a distillery visit because I had a few jobs to do aboard, but I did find some automatic transmission fluid as well as some more ginger beer. I got into a conversation with a man in one of the shops about the whiskies – apparently there are seven distilleries in all – and he recommended the smoky Caol Ila, one of the less well-known Islay malts. He also encouraged me to make a visit to where it's made, more for the views than anything else; apparently the place was totally rebuilt in the 1970s but it nestles in one of the most wildly picturesque spots in Islay. Now I'm only an occasional whisk(e)y drinker and two bottles would probably last me not just for the voyage but for the year (and that includes guests), but I like having a choice in the drinks locker, Islay malts are among my favourites, and it wouldn't do to be sailing around Scotland with Bushmills as the sole representative of the ilk.

I never did visit the distillery or return to the shop for a bottle. By the time I'd finished my chores aboard *Indalo* it was already early evening and I was getting hungry. One of the two eating-places in the village was fully booked leaving just the Maharani, in good Port Ellen fashion the strangest Indian restaurant I've ever been in (and again I'm not complaining). I was asked to go and buy my own bottle of drink which isn't so unusual, and while I was at it to bring back half a gallon of milk, which I thought is. The furniture and decor were basic and the establishment might have been a 'caff' not long ago (like lunchtime), but the food was good.

Next morning the weather forecast said fresh south-westerlies and heavy showers, but outside the overnight rainfall had given way to flat calm and thick mist. Now I'd got a toehold in Scotland I wanted to move on up to Crinan and Oban, so I decided that unless the visibility grew worse I'd set out. An hour later I could see across the bay, but the day was cold and dank so I donned my heaviest assortment of clothes yet: T-shirt, rugby shirt, jumper, thick fleece, and waterproofs including the chest-high trousers that are very good at keeping water out but also make passing it a major operation. Plus scarf, gauntlet gloves and lifejacket, and boots with thick socks. Feeling a bit like a Michelin man I slipped my ropes at 0730 and trickled out of the harbour, motoring peacefully through the mist and out past Islay's rocky south-eastern corner before turning up into the Sound of Jura.

The mist was never thick enough to be a problem, but it did justify my choice of apparel and more to the point spoiled what should have been a spectacular passage along the Sound and past the mountains called the Paps of Jura. For the first few miles I was alone, but before long some other vessels began to appear: a fishing boat with a diver down, a trawler, and then a ferry plying between the mainland and Jura. There were no other yachts in sight but a little further north I picked up a pan-pan call on the VHF. Pan-pan is what's called an urgency call, and it's used when a boat needs help but vessel or lives aren't in immediate danger. A yacht had been leaving an anchorage on Jura and on its way out it had run aground on some rocks that are clearly marked on the chart. The tide was rising so it would eventually lift off, but in the meantime the skipper was worried about the hull getting damaged. Clyde Coastguard came on the air to co-ordinate, another yacht that had just left the anchorage turned back and a fishing boat headed in. The casualty was gently eased off the rocks and escorted to a mooring buoy, all ending happily.

A little further up the sound from where the incident occurred I passed Skervuile lighthouse in midstream, the visibility now much better with a hint of sun in the background. There were good views of the coast to both sides, but the Paps were still determined not to emerge from their covering of mist. Next the lighthouse of Ruabh Sgeir came into view marking the centre of the sound and the beginning of my run into Crinan. It was only two in the afternoon as I turned into the loch and I could have happily continued to Oban, except that the tide would have met me coming the other way down the Sound of Luing. I briefly explored the loch, more a deep bay than what I'd normally think of as a sea-loch, then I tied up to a spare mooring buoy and put the kettle on.

At Crinan I was rejoining my planned route from Port St Mary. If I'd sailed north to Portpatrick I would have stopped off at Troon or Ardrossan in the Forth of Clyde before continuing to Lamlash on Arran, and eventually arrived at Ardrishaig where the Crinan Canal cuts its picturesque course across the Kintyre peninsula. Then after a day of working locks and gentle motoring I would have emerged here in this stunning setting at Crinan. The harbour appears completely surrounded by steep hills, pine-clad slopes and rocky outcrops, and the lack of a view to the open sea makes it seem more like a stretch of river than a sea-loch. Most of the boats swing to buoys rather than being tied to pontoons or quays, a reminder of the Yealm or the Helford though in other respects the scene is quintessentially Scottish. Added to that the afternoon sun had finally driven off the mist, and though I'd removed all but two layers of clothing I was still warm. The water was millpond-calm, *Indalo* sat peacefully to her buoy, and I opened all the hatches and lazed in the cockpit in a midsummer idyll.

The weather and the scenery put me in such a good mood that I decided to do a job I'd been putting off since leaving Wales. The toilet had slowly developed a leak, making it necessary to mop out and clean the heads compartment at first daily and then after every use. After I detached the china bowl from the plumbing and unbolted it from the floor I found a crack in its base. It really needed a new toilet or at least a new base, but for now I made a temporary repair and stuck everything together with lots of mastic. I'd keep a bucket handy until the morning and hope the mastic would do the job. After spending what remained of the afternoon cleaning mastic off my hands and disinfecting just about everything I put together a meal of tinned chilli and boiled rice with chopped fruit and vegetables. Eating in the cockpit to escape the Savlon-steeped cabin I relaxed with a glass of Portuguese red and enjoyed the warm and peaceful summer evening .

Sunday's passage to Oban involved some of the most challenging navigation yet. It would include two swift and potentially dangerous stretches of water, first the brief but fast-flowing bottleneck of the Dorus Mòr or Great Gate, then the main passage northwards through the tumultuous Sound of Luing. Between the two are some hidden rocks to miss and further on there's a confusing patch of shallows in Kerrera Sound on the run in to Oban. What's more at certain states of tide a strong stream sets westwards from the Dorus Mòr into the fearsome Gulf of Corryvreckan, a narrow stretch of water between the northern tip of Jura and the tall, round island of Scarba. As the tide ebbs down the Sound of Jura the water drops half a metre below the level to seaward and the ocean outside cascades through the Corryvreckan to make up the difference. When there's a strong wind in the opposite direction standing waves build up like walls of water, and to complete the picture the current swirls around an underwater outcrop to create one of the world's most spectacular whirlpools. One Eric Blair, better known as the author George Orwell, nearly drowned here when his boat overturned and he was stranded on a rock. Fortunately perhaps there's not really any good navigational reason to transit the Corryvreckan. Declan, who saw me off at the beginning of the voyage, once did it in a sea kayak.

The timing of the passage is critical to pass through the Great Gate at slack water and from there carry the tide up through the Sound of Luing. Slack was half-past eight, so I slipped my mooring at 0800 under an overcast sky and still air. Pilotage through the Dorus Mòr was a doddle, the water was flat calm and even the Corryvreckan looked benign. I passed close to a small islet called Reisa an t-Sruith to clear some offlying rocks further north, took a bearing on the summit of Scarba and turned northwards for the Sound of Luing. By now I was picking up some tide and in less than an hour *Indalo* came safely through the northern end of the Sound between the twin lights of Fladda and Dubh Sgeir. I took some photographs of the little settlement of Ellanbeich on the island of Seil, then turned on to a northeasterly course between Seil and Insh to make for Kerrera.

Like yesterday there was some action on the airwaves, a pan-pan call from a yacht far to the south about an upturned motor dory, deadpan reply from Clyde Coastguard. The yacht had rescued the dory's lone occupant but couldn't turn the boat the right way up. I lost the yacht's signal shortly after so I was left listening to a one-sided conversation, but the from what I could make out the boat was towed still inverted into the safety of a loch where assistance was at hand.

The entrance to Kerrera Sound could easily be the mouth of a river, though in reality it's simply a stretch of water between the island and the mainland, open at both ends. Halfway up is the shallow patch I mentioned earlier, marked by some red and green buoys arranged to test the visiting mariner's pilotage skills. It all makes sense after looking at the chart: the shallows are in the middle with deeper water to either side, so to take the deeper, right-hand channel keep the red buoys to port as you would coming in to a river. The island itself measures about eight miles by two and has forty residents, a hostel and a tea shop, and there's a boatyard with a small marina at Ardantrive at the northern end. The far end of the sound opens out into Oban Bay, with the busy port of Oban on the right and Ardantrive to the left. Though there are a few mooring buoys in various other parts of the bay Ardantrive is the main yacht berthing facility for Oban and there's a free passenger ferry connecting the two.

I berthed at Ardantrive and made use of the marina's excellent facilities, which went some of the way towards compensating for it being expensive. Oban Yachts who run the place also have a marine engineering operation and advertise that they can order all sorts of chandlery, so I asked without much hope if they could find me a Jabsco Par toilet, small bowl version with manual pump, post haste. Yes was the reply after a phone call and fax to check the specification, by lunchtime tomorrow.

My two-day stay in Oban was subject to sun and showers in about equal measure, but at last the good weather was beginning to get the upper hand. I made a short foray into the town on the first evening but it rained heavily and I didn't see very much other than the inside of the Oban Inn. The next day was brighter after a showery start, ideal for exploring. I picked up a rather nice pictorial map in the tourist office, found the station, got my bearings among the shops and had lunch at a modern Scottish-Italian bistro on the quay. I'd only ever visited Oban briefly, and that ten years ago when I stopped overlooking the harbour for half an hour before continuing southwards by car. This time I got a much better impression of the place as a bustling but friendly holiday resort, port and regional centre. Ferries were constantly arriving and departing, trip and fishing boats were going about their business, and the views across the bay and over to the steep shores of Mull were bordering on the sublime.

Resisting the temptations of the Oban Distillery I took a climb up to McCaig's Tower or Folly, a curious colosseum-type structure above the northern side of the harbour that forms something of a landmark when approaching the harbour. It was begun in 1890 by local businessman and philanthropist J S McCaig with the intention of it becoming a museum and art gallery, in the meantime providing work for builders and stonemasons during the quieter winter months. Ten years later the outer wall had been completed at a cost of £5000, but McCaig died soon after and work stopped leaving the tower as a shell much as it is today. A public garden has been laid out inside somehow emphasising that it's just a high wall; but the walk was worth it for the views across the bay and over to the islands, framed by the tower's 'windows.'

After walking out of town as far as the ruined twelfth-century Dunollie Castle, I returned via the coast road and took a look in the little 'war and peace' museum by the quay. Just one small room, it was full of World War II relics and stories including some displays about Oban's role as a base for Sunderland flying boats. It was fascinating, and I could have stopped longer except that despite the early hour it was about to close. At least there was enough time left to do some shopping: a Scottish courtesy flag from Nancy Black's chandlery, a bottle of cask-strength Caol Ila from the whisky shop, a few provisions from the supermarket, and a Para Handy book from Ottakar's to provide some nautical reading appropriate to the west coast. For those who haven't come across him Para Handy is a fictional puffer skipper who plied the Clyde estuary and the ports of western Scotland at the beginning of the twentieth century. Neil Munro originally wrote the stories as newspaper columns, so they are short but many. Gently humorous and written in dialect they describe the various adventures and scrapes of the small crew of the steamer or puffer *Vital Spark*, capturing a way of life now long gone when these little steamships transported supplies around the western seaboard.

Back at the marina I collected the toilet and stowed it away in the quarterberth for attention on a rainy day. Walking along the pontoon I was hailed by fellow round-Britain yachtsman Keith from *Dart Dash*, a Contessa 32 based like me in Dartmouth, who had spotted my Devon flag and came over to introduce himself. He explained that he intended to take the short-cut through the Caledonian Canal and Loch Ness rather than brave the wilds of the far north, so wrongly as things were to turn out I expected he would get well ahead of me. Shortly afterwards I started talking to some other neighbours who I'd met briefly on the ferry. Called Jim and Joan, they were over from Strangford Lough with *Tamaray*, their Cornish Rustler 36. There were three Rustlers visiting the marina and I let myself be talked into attending an impromptu owner's club meeting on one of them complete with wine, whisky and snacks.

Tuesday looked to be a fine day so I decided to move on to Tobermory on the Isle of Mull. I'd just read an article in *Practical Boat Owner* by Roger Oliver, who completed a single-handed circuit of Britain in 2002 followed two years later by another of Britain and Ireland. In this month's episode he was on the west coast of Scotland and he described the stretch from Oban to Tobermory as the most scenic passage of his entire voyage. With good visibility and a fair breeze from the south I was looking forward to following in his footsteps. So I refuelled, left the harbour with the sails up and waited for an incoming Calmac ferry to clear the entrance. Once it had passed I set a course for Lady Rock, an islet that marks the passage between the long thin island of Lismore and the steep-sided bulk of Mull. There was a fresh breeze coming across the beam and I had hoisted full sail, so *Indalo* flew. The speed through the water increased to 6.5, 7, and finally 7.5 knots with only a steadying hand on the tiller. Exhilarating stuff. Not to last though: as I came up to my turn at Lady Rock and eased out the sails to run up the coast of Mull the wind dropped and so did my speed, enough to call for the engine. This was to be the story all the way: foresail in, engine on, foresail out, engine off, and so on. In this fashion I cleared the Grey Rocks at the entrance to the Sound of Mull and worked my way up the sound past Lochaline, Ardnacross, Glenmorven. There were plenty of other yachts doing the same, but it was the last time I would see more than a couple of sails in the same stretch of water for several hundred miles.

The Sound was scenic but not to my mind spectacular, and I'd argue with Roger that the Antrim coast was more dramatic. Tobermory though I would have to agree about. I picked up a buoy in Tobermory bay that had a panoramic view of the village front. The lower row of houses, shops and inns are painted in many colours, freshly painted too courtesy of the children's TV series *Balamory*. A second more subdued row runs along the hillside higher up, and the whole effect is rather cosy and picturesque. Tobermory is the capital or main settlement of Mull, but to put things in perspective it's home to only 750 people, about half the size of Hugh Town on St Mary's in the Isles of Scilly. Continuing the comparison, Mull is twice the size of the Isle of Wight but its population at two and a half thousand is about the same as that of the whole of Scilly. Despite the figures Tobermory has an impressive range of eating and drinking places and a fair selection of shops, not all of them selling Balamory goods (or maybe I didn't look hard enough). It's a magnet for visiting yachts and for tourists, but it's kept plenty of its charm nonetheless.

I pumped the dinghy up and went ashore to take a look around, briefly exploring the village before calling in at the Mishnish Hotel or 'Mish' as it's known locally. Recommended in the pilot book as *the* place for water-borne visitors it's an unspoilt old inn with three main bars and several cosy side rooms. Although it was late June a warm fire was going in one of the bars, maybe because the locals knew better than to share my new-found optimism about the weather. After having a beer there I decided to go somewhere else to eat, simply to see what was around, and ended up in a place I'd seen earlier called Posh Nosh. It wasn't, but it was better than it sounded. Finally I called in at a bar close to the yacht quay to sample the Tobermory malt, lost a pair of glasses in the sea (nothing to do with the whisky) and rowed home. Tobermory (or Tobar Mhoire) means Mary's Well or Mary's Spring, and if I've got the Gaelic right Bala Mhoire is Mary's Ball.

Overnight it rained almost incessantly. Though the morning was better the wind had gone to a fresh to strong northerly, not ideal for the next passage. I'd half resolved to stay in Tobermory anyway. First on my list was changing the toilet, much easier than doing the repair, then the navigation up to Kyleakin on Skye. If the weather was OK on Friday morning I could make a start at the crack of dawn, anchor for three or four hours in Isleornsay or Loch Hourn to wait for the tide

through the narrows of Kyle Rhea, then push on for a late afternoon arrival. Otherwise it would be two passages with a
stop at Armadale or Isleornsay. But at the moment the forecast was still for fresh northerlies so I suspected I might be in
Tobermory until the weekend.

After lunch I took the dinghy ashore again and looked in
at the little Mull museum to brush up my knowledge about
the island. Mull's present shape, something like a letter M on
its side, emerged about ten thousand years ago when the
glaciers retreated at the end of the last Ice Age, and the island
is something of a geologist's paradise because it consists of
several different layers of rock superimposed over each other.
Moving forward a few millennia Tobermory itself didn't
really come into being until 1788 when what was known as
British Harbour was constructed with a partly planned
village around it. The idea had been to establish a fishing
port, but the best fishing grounds were too far away and
instead it became a trading and ferry harbour, wartime naval
training base, and finally a major (in Hebridean terms
anyway) yachting centre.

The naval connection was that during World War II
Tobermory Bay accommodated HMS *Western Isles*, the base
for working up escort ships for convoys and training their
crews of reservists and new recruits. Over eleven hundred
ships and 200,000 men began their service there under
Commodore Gilbert Stevenson, known as the Terror of
Tobermory for his strict efficiency. One of the less fortunate
legacies of this highly necessary wartime work is that the sea
bed is littered with discarded cables, chains and other debris,
making anchoring an interesting experience. Also on the
bottom is a Spanish Armada ship called the *San Juan de Sicilia*,
part of the fleet that was swept in 1588 up the North Sea and
around the north coast of Scotland. It took refuge in
Tobermory only to sink when a fire on board ignited its
munitions. For a hundred and fifty years the ship was visible
below the surface, and rumours of a cargo of treasure have

lured divers and speculators from the eighteenth century onwards. The last salvage attempt was in 1982, but so far the only Spanish Treasure to be found on Mull is a local beer.

Having been in Australia a couple of years back my eye was drawn to a small exhibit about Lachlan Macquarie, who both grew up and spent his final years on Mull and has a small mausoleum on the road to Salen. Macquarie is hardly known in his native country but in south-east Australia his name is unmissable. A one-time general who had been stationed for much of his service in India, he was appointed in 1810 as governor of New South Wales to succeed the controversial William Bligh of *Bounty* fame. He instituted a vast number of public works and by all accounts was a humane and capable administrator who saw the colony as an emerging community rather than as a penal settlement. Although he made enemies enough to force his resignation after eleven years in office, his legacy is remembered in features that would fill the index of an atlas: there's a Macquarie River, Macquarie Island, some Macquarie Hills and Macquarie Plains, Macquarie Falls, a Macquarie Pass, Point Macquarie, Fort Macquarie, Macquarie University, Macquarie Bank, Macquarie Grove Aerodrome and Mrs Macquarie's Seat to name just a few, as well as the more mundane Macquarie Cafés, Streets and Stores and a few Lachlan Streets too. Sadly, Lachlan himself had little time to enjoy his retirement back in Mull and died in 1824 from an illness that had dogged him since his military days.

After the museum I wanted to have a look around the distillery, but I'd missed the last tour so I bought some ingredients for dinner and looked for a coffee shop for a coffee instead. The two I found had both closed, but I had better luck in the bar where I'd sampled the whisky the night before. A character sitting in a dark corner waved me over: it turned out to be Jim from *Tamaray*. Joan returned from shopping for some Balamory mementoes, then we had a chat over coffees and beers. I was gently chided for not visiting

Strangford Lough on my way up the Irish coast, and invited to call in if I was ever in that direction again.

Friday morning started fair if still a bit breezy for the passage north. I rowed back over to the dinghy pontoon, showered in the Mishnish, took a walk into the upper part of the village, and finally returned to the hotel for a lunch of haggis and salad. By now the wind had dropped a little, and sitting at the pub window the weather looked so good it was a pity not to be at sea. So I finished my lunch, rowed back and finalised my passage plan. If all went well I could leave at half-past two on the tide and get into Isleornsay or nearby Loch na Dal before dark, continuing up to Kyleakin early the next day. If not I'd made notes for entering Drumbuie and Kilchoan on the south side of the Ardnamurchan peninsula, harbours on the islands of Rhum, Muck and Eigg, Armadale at the southern end of Skye, and Mallaig on the mainland opposite.

With a clipboard full of waterproof pilotage notes I set off as planned and had a cracking sail out past the north coast of Mull and along the steep southern edge of Ardnamurchan, the long 'nose' of Scotland, towards Ardnamurchan Point. Ardnamurchan is the westernmost point of the British mainland, a broad, blunt headland with a lighthouse to mark its tip. It doesn't have the strong currents or offlying rocks of the Cornish or Welsh extremities but it needs to be treated with respect nevertheless. Traditionally boats that pass north around Ardnamurchan earn the right to wear a bunch of heather on their bowsprits, though whether they should have some ready to hand for the passage or are supposed to forage for it at the next landfall I didn't know.

Ardnamurchan Point and its lighthouse came into view gradually, and disappeared gradually while the mountains of Mull receded astern. As I altered course towards the distant Sound of Sleat, the passage between Skye and the mainland, the wind came directly on to *Indalo*'s nose. I made the best course I could under sail pointing towards the island of Muck, tacked southeastwards for a couple of miles, then turned back again to the north. There wasn't much tide and I wasn't going anywhere fast: barely three knots in the direction I wanted. Reluctantly I put the engine on and steered into the wind. The three 'small isles' were now off to port: first Muck, small and flat, then Eigg with its cockscomb lava peak, and then in the distance Rhum (or Rum), tall and stately with its steep double head in the clouds. The wind was now moderate to fresh which would have been ideal if I'd been going in any other direction but northeast. Waves were crashing against Indalo's bow, erupting into spray and washing up the deck. Even with the engine cranked up I was only making four knots, well off cruising speed, and I was getting regular showers from the spray. I considered turning off to Rhum and anchoring in Loch Scresort, but once Eigg was to port it seemed a long diversion for little gain.

As soon as I'd passed Eigg the waves grew longer and the wind moved enough to the north to fill the mainsail, so I for the moment I had a faster and more comfortable passage across to Skye. I was soon tucked under the island's southern tip, but instead of providing shelter the land funnelled the wind down towards me and increased its strength. The waves went back to a short chop and every one sent spray flying and water cascading up the deck. Plus the tide was turning. It was already nine o'clock as I drew parallel with Mallaig, and Isleornsay was another two hours to go. Not wanting to enter in darkness I motored over to the Skye side to see if Armadale was tenable.

Several yachts were already moored off Armadale and they looked secure if animated by the swell. If I moored up now I could get my head down fairly quickly, ready for an 0300 start the next day. So I steered for the nearest buoy, read a plastic card attached to it to make sure it was for visitors, and promptly missed it with the boathook. My second attempt was better but I caught the boathook in the rigging and by the time I'd disentangled it the main buoy had gone down one side of the boat and a small pick-up buoy attached to it by a long length of thin rope disappeared down the other. No problem, I'll just drift clear and have another go. I waited, but nothing happened: the rope must have snagged underneath. The main buoy was at the stern of the boat next to the cockpit, so I reached over and tied a rope on it. Just at that moment my knee knocked the engine into gear, wrapping the pick-up rope tightly around the propeller. I tried putting the engine in ahead to unwind the rope but it just struggled, so I put it back into neutral and switched it off. I cursed roundly. There was no way out of this now that didn't involve getting wet.

I went below for a quick drink and a cheese sandwich while I decided what to do. *Indalo* was tied up safely so there was no danger, only the prospect of a dip in the cold sea. Down south I'd probably have stripped off and jumped in, but here the water was colder and a dip in the sea didn't appeal. Though it would be slightly more tricky because the boat was bouncing about on the waves rather than in a calm marina, I'd try the same method I'd used in Ballycastle. I donned a makeshift immersion suit and my one manually-operated lifejacket, then inflated the dinghy and tied it in position at the port quarter. I let some air out of one of the tubes and used my left arm to protect my head from the hull, while with my free hand I groped around underneath. After some unpicking of knots the pick-up buoy bobbed to the surface, then I unravelled the rest of the rope. Job done, but I still had to deflate the dinghy, re-attach the pickup buoy, walk the mooring buoy down to the bows of the boat, and change out of my wet upper clothes. By the time I'd dried myself off, had a cup of tea and broken out the Caol Ila it was nearly midnight. I gave up on the early morning start and crawled into my sleeping bag for a welcome rest, *Indalo* rolling and banging in the waves.

In the morning there was still something of a swell coming into Armadale, though the wind had dropped to a gentle whisper. It was too late to leave for Kyleakin because the tide was about to turn and up at the narrows of Kylerhea it would be running at nearly six knots. I could though move the eight miles to Isleornsay or Loch na Dal, where things would be calmer. As I slipped the mooring and made my way up the Sound of Sleat everything was calm and peaceful, letting me appreciate the rugged mountains on Skye to the left and Knoydart across to the right. Loch Hourn opened up on the mainland side, and on the Skye shore I motored carefully around Isleornsay into the entrance of Loch na Dal, noting a small lighthouse and a beacon marking some offlying rocks. Isleornsay has a rather attractive natural harbour between the islet and the eponymous village on the Skye mainland, and today it was well protected from the swell. Finding a clear spot I put down my anchor to await the turn of the tide.

After catching up on some sleep I ate a civilised lunch in the cockpit while taking in the surroundings. It's here that the author, conservationist and one-time Special Forces instructor Gavin Maxwell wrote *Ring of Bright Water* before moving to Eilean Bàn in Kyle Akin. The sun had come out, Isleornsay looked idyllic, and the passage through Kyle Rhea beckoned. The Sound of Sleat narrows from three miles at Isleornsay down to a mile in the approach to the kyle, and finally to a bare half-mile until it emerges at the marine equivalent of a T-junction in Loch Alsh. The current increases as the water's funnelled in to the narrows, so it's important to get the timing right and do the pilotage properly to avoid being swept off course and put aground. I set off at three in the afternoon and entered Kyle Rhea just as the tide turned in my favour. The upper end of the Sound of Sleat is a dramatic mix of mountains and glens and the approach to the kyle has the feeling of disappearing into a narrow gorge, both *Indalo* and the tiny hamlet of Kylerhea itself becoming insignificant against the grandeur of the mountains. Like the Sound of

Luing and the Dorus Mòr the pilotage wasn't as difficult as it looked on the chart: steer at the rounded hill until a beacon comes into view, keep a compass bearing on the beacon, turn to starboard just before reaching it and then head for the centre of the kyle to escape the shallows to port.

At the head of Kyle Rhea the great panorama that is Loch Alsh opened up in front of me, a spectacular bowl of water with sweeping mountain views in every direction. Turning westwards into the wind I dropped the sails ready for the run in to Kyle Akin. This kyle is the last relatively narrow stretch of water before the passage between Skye and the mainland widens out into the more open waters that eventually become the Inner Sound. There's a choice to be made here, marked by some islets in midstream: the northern, mainland bank and the little town of Kyle of Lochalsh, or the southern one and the village of Kyleakin, until the coming of the bridge Skye's main ferry port. My choice was swayed by the pilot book, a recommendation from Geoff from *High Potential* who had passed this way a week or more earlier, and a natural predilection for islands. I came south of the islets, spotted what appeared to be the blasted stump of a gigantic tree on a hillock, and turned in to Kyleakin's little harbour to tie up.

6

From Haakon's Kyle to Thor's River

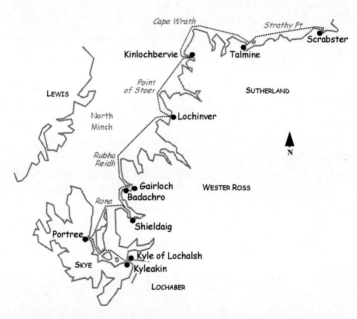

I took an immediate liking to Kyleakin the settlement as well as to Kyle Akin the stretch of water. The village isn't as picturesque as Tobermory but it manages to blend old harbourside cottages, 1950s semis and modern buildings of different styles in a way that just works, and this in a stunning, expansive setting of hills, heather and sea that's the equal of anything in Britain. Even the Skye bridge adds to the scene, arching gracefully from Skye across to the islet of

Eilean Bàn then continuing as a causeway to the mainland. At one time much of the road traffic arriving on Skye would have come through Kyleakin, but now it passes the village by without a thought. The loss of passing trade may have affected the shops, but there still seem to be plenty of visitors to fill the hotels, hostels, holiday cottages and guest houses.

Kyle Akin, Caol Acain in Gaelic, is so-named because the Norwegian king Haakon anchored his fleet in the narrows there on his way to (or according to some versions from, or it might have been both) the Battle of Largs in 1263. Haakon was overlord of much of the north and west of Scotland, which had been ruled from Norway since the ninth century. His long reign was mostly one of peace and prosperity but towards its end his sovereignty of the Western Isles was challenged by Alexander III of Scotland. To repel the Scots Haakon set out with a force of a hundred and twenty ships supported by a smaller navy raised by his Manx allies, only to run into a gale in the Clyde that scattered the fleet and drove part of it ashore. Taking advantage of the Norwegians' disarray Alexander engaged them at Largs. The battle was indecisive and both sides claimed it as a victory, but whatever the truth of the matter the Scots came out with the upper hand and three years later Haakon's successor formally handed over the islands in the Treaty of Perth. Haakon himself died from illness or battle wounds on Orkney as his fleet made its way home.

I felt at ease on reaching Kyleakin. Apart from the ambience of the place and the good weather I was well ahead of schedule and had only one more short passage to do to arrive at my rendezvous with Chris, veteran of some cross-Channel and west of Cornwall passages and my crew for the north coast, in a week's time. After the delays earlier in the voyage I'd harboured a few private doubts about getting all the way around, but now with the north coast only three or four short sailing days away they were all gone and the passage up to Cape Wrath and across to the Pentland Firth was laid out in my mind's eye. As well as looking forward to some company on passage I had friends to visit on both the west and the east sides of Scotland, and if that wasn't enough, summer had finally broken through.

In that frame of mind I took a short stroll around the village, found myself actually enjoying browsing the shelves of a gift shop, and then walked around the back of the shop to stumble on Haakon's Bar. Haakon's is an architecturally drab and scruffily furnished place that like the gift shop appealed to me against all logic. Obviously set up for the hostel trade, it has a canteen-style restaurant that does straightforward and cheap but good food. I ate some of it then took another walk down to the bridgeward end of the village, returning along the water's edge and climbing to the top of a small hill with a memorial and some good views over the harbour. Finding a westward-facing bench I sat and wrote out some postcards as the light faded into the brief northern night.

Next morning I set out to explore the area a little more and take in the views. I strolled around the harbour, walked past some attractive old cottages and some newer bungalows, and picked my way across the foreshore and up a hill to the object I'd mistaken for a giant tree stump. It was a stone ruin called Castle Moil or Dun Haakon, not particularly note-worthy in itself though it did provide some excellent views of Kyleakin framed against the Skye bridge. According to tradition it was built around 900 by a Norwegian princess who is remembered locally as Saucy Mary. Among other things she was said to have had a chain stretched across the kyle so that she could levy a toll on any ships that wanted to pass. Until recently this was dismissed as something of a myth, because the technology of the day wouldn't have been up to making a chain half a mile long that could be pulled taut without breaking. In fact the 'chain' was probably a string of old ships roped together, which makes much better sense as a toll-barrier and would be easier to defend against anyone intent on forcing their way through.

From the castle I made an assault on the hill to the east of the village, but the paths proved too peaty and waterlogged for my footwear. So I skirted the hill on rough paths through heather and gorse before coming down by a small bridge at the back of the harbour. I carried on past Kyleakin's smart new community centre and turned right to cross the Skye bridge to Kyle of Lochalsh (or simply 'Kyle' as it's known locally). Part of the way across an official green mileage board told me I was on the A87, but the rest was in Gaelic: I worked out Caol Loch Ailse and Inbhir Nis soon enough, Am Ploc translates to Plockton and Balle Mac Ara is just Balmacara, but An Gearasdan defeated me. Just beyond the sign the main span of the bridge rises to nearly a hundred feet above the water and provides commanding and panoramic views down Loch Alsh on one side and out to Raasay and the Inner Sound on the other. Then it descends to Gavin Maxwell's islet of Eilean Bàn and looks over the roof of what used to be his house, before continuing on the level across to the mainland. I walked into Kyle, had a look around the town, and paid 15p for a bus back across the bridge to Kyleakin.

On Monday I visited the Bright Water Visitor Centre opposite the pontoon where I was moored. It's run by a charity called the Eilean Bàn Trust, an offshoot of the better-known Born Free Foundation. The Foundation was formed by actors Virginia McKenna and Bill Travers who starred in the film version of *Ring of Bright Water*, and after the bridge was built in 1995 it intervened with the Scottish Office to secure Eilean Bàn as a nature reserve. Though the centre was geared to younger visitors it was interesting enough to leave me thinking that one of their guided tours of Eilean Bàn would have been worthwhile.

Later on I moved *Indalo* across to Kyle to refuel, shop and take on water. The town is less atmospheric than its smaller neighbour, though it's attractive enough in its own way and it has a compact centre with a sprinkling of shops and hostelries as well as a well-stocked 'out-of-town' (by which I mean a couple of hundred yards) Co-Op supermarket. It still has the feel of a ferry port, with a period railway station beside the quay that conjures up the noise and smell of steam trains and the bustle of hundreds of visitors arriving with their suitcases to catch the boat across to Skye. The trains still arrive but onward travel is now by bus or taxi and there's a feel of being cheated slightly to arrive on the quayside only to be whisked away again by road.

My last job for the day was to check out transport connections for Chris, who would be arriving at Inverness (sorry, Inbhir Nis) on Friday. We were planning to meet at Shieldaig, but I noticed that there was a better bus connection to Gairloch and emailed him to meet me there. I could go to Portree tomorrow, then Shieldaig for a couple of days, and on to Gairloch on Friday morning. Pleased with the logistics I treated myself to a meal in the big and somewhat grand-looking Lochalsh Hotel for dinner. It wasn't quite as grand or luxurious as its appearance promised, but the food was very acceptable and the seats in the conservatory overlooked the boats coming and going on the yacht pontoon.

Tuesday opened in silver mist suffused with a hint of golden sun. Expecting the gold to get the upper hand by mid-morning I prepared leisurely to catch the tide at noon. Portree is just over twenty miles from Kyle, a passage in two parts: the first under Skye bridge, between the islands of Longay and Scalpay and across to the broad southern end of Raasay, and the second a short dogleg through the Caol Mòr towards Skye and then north through the Narrows of Raasay and around the corner to Portree. I slipped my ropes at 1130 and passed under the bridge in a hazy flat calm. As the arching span receded into the distance I started to close with the small islands, flat Pabay first off to the south, then compact, rocky Longay and opposite it the imposing domed island of Scalpay. The sun finally chased the mist away and I was soon down to T-shirt, shorts and bare feet, admiring the view as the autopilot did the steering. The passage was already rivalling Saturday's as the most beautiful yet. There were rolling hills and islands everywhere, the sun was glinting on the sea, and the pines on Pabay hinted at something subtropical. A small red-sailed yawl crept out from Skye and headed towards Scalpay, and a little further on a landing-craft ferry left the pier at Suisnish Point on Raasay, did a pirouette and crossed over to the bigger island.

The next part of the passage took me past the bucolic settlements of Inverarish and Clachan on the Raasay side and the tall grandeur of Ben Lee on Skye opposite. Beyond the Narrows I turned a few points to starboard to round mighty Ben Tianavaig, the great rock that protects the entrance to Portree. Coming from the south there's no sign that there's a harbour or a settlement here until the gap leading to Portree Loch opens up and reveals the town a couple of miles behind the entrance. I steered in, passed a line of rocks and its marker buoy to starboard, and picked up a mooring in the outer part of the harbour. Then it was up with the dinghy and into Port Rígh, King's Port, the main settlement on Skye and the place that James V chose to assert his authority over the fiercely independent local chieftains in 1540.

I'd visited Portree by car a few years back, staying on the harbour front in a guest house that allowed yacht crews to use the showers. My impression then as now was of a bustling, businesslike little town, another place that had managed to blend old and new successfully. The harbour front is on a par with Tobermory, but once past the first row of houses it's clear that this is more a working island capital than a pretty resort. I had some items of hardware to buy for the boat, so as Portree was the biggest settlement I expected to visit until Thurso or Wick I made some quick enquiries and headed off to a trading estate on the edge of town before everything closed. Walking through the business end of

Portree reinforced my impressions about the town. It is home to around two thousand people and it's big enough to have a small suburb, an industrial estate, a hospital, a secondary school and a public swimming pool. Given that Skye is bigger than some English counties it's not surprising that its capital is a well-equipped little place. Though the bridge has brought easier access to the mainland it hasn't changed the fact that Oban, Inbhir Nis and even Fort William (An Gearasden, The Fort or Garrison, so now I know) are all a long way off.

Returning from the trading estate I searched for a pub with an outside table where I could sit and cool down with a cold beer. I couldn't find one, but I did find McNab's Inn next to the Royal Hotel. McNab's was where Bonnie Prince Charlie once said farewell to Flora Macdonald, but since then it had been converted to a modern lounge bar and a tasteful café-style eating area, both light and airy if to my mind more Edinburgh than Skye. But the beer was both local and good and the food perfectly acceptable too.

Before going back on board I called in at the guest house where I'd stayed. A woman answered the door and explained that they were now semi-retired, only let a couple of rooms, and didn't have spare showers any more. I didn't recollect her although I would have remembered her husband, who was out for the evening. I'd chatted with him about sailing into Portree one day and it would have been nice to let him know I'd actually done it. I checked my rucksack but I'd not brought any *Indalo* bookmarks with me, so I just asked her to pass on my best wishes.

The following morning started hot and sunny with a gentle breeze from the east and something of a haze out to sea. After paying my dues I prepared the dinghy for towing, hoisted the mainsail, slipped the mooring and motored out of the harbour between Ben Tianavaig to starboard and the equally dramatic cliffs of Torvaig to port. There wasn't enough wind to sail so I set the autopilot to steer north-northeast across the Sound of Raasay and clear the northern tip of Rona. To the west loomed the steep coast of the Trotternish peninsula, and to the east Raasay and its offlying islands appeared like a set of cardboard cut-outs silhouetted in the haze.

After clearing Rona and turning eastwards towards Loch Torridon I spotted a minke whale surfacing lazily in the distance, followed by a coaster on my port side that seemed intent on racing me into the loch. I gunned the engine to keep clear of it, but before our courses converged it turned off for the village of Diabaig to do business with the salmon farm. Turning to starboard I passed through some narrows into Loch Shieldaig, ignoring the easterly extension to Loch Torridon that leads up to Torridon village. From seaward Shieldaig itself appears as a string of houses on a narrow strip of land between the water's edge and the great bulk of Ben Shieldaig behind. Approaching the village carefully to avoid a shoal patch I crept in behind the heavily wooded Shieldaig Island and approached the shallow, protected anchorage that was my destination.

Dropping the anchor in the appointed place and checking that it had dug in securely, I took the dinghy ashore. My friend Karen had been unsure when she would be arriving home so I called at the local inn to wait while I had a pint and a leisurely dinner of some locally-caught fish. There was still no sign of her when I'd finished my meal, so I went for a walk around the village in what was now becoming fine mizzle. Above Shieldaig is the through road that hugs the mountainside and takes most of the traffic. The village sits on a loop that descends to the loch, runs along the shore, turns inland again then rejoins the main route maybe half a mile further on. I followed the circuit around clockwise and emerged at the upper end of the loch, spotting a man who was watching something through a pair of binoculars. He told me he had been looking at an otter which I'd probably scared away. We got talking about the village and about boats, then it turned out he was a fisherman so we moved on to fishing. As long as you weren't out to get rich it seemed perfectly possible to make a living from *fruits de mer* up here, though some big companies and trawlers from the east coast had recently tried to muscle in. After generations of gentlemen's agreements about who can fish where and for what, it seemed that Shieldaig was about to enter an age of more legalistic arrangements.

Karen didn't appear until I'd given up and returned aboard, but next morning I took the dinghy back across to meet her for a breakfast-time coffee and, after she had left for the day, the luxury of a relaxing soak in the bath. Next I called in at the guest house I'd stayed in on my last visit to the village. It was run by a friend of Karen's, an Englishman called Trevor who had been most welcoming and cooked good enough breakfasts to tempt me out of my normal habit of refusing hot food before the sun's over the yardarm. Though I'd only stayed for two or three days and he'd been out of action for the past year he remembered me, and we had a chat over another coffee in his lounge before he went off to help out at the school. My final call for the morning was the well-stocked shop, where I bought some fresh ingredients so I could invite Karen on board for a meal.

Later in the day I took a more leisurely walk around the village. It takes time to switch into the pace of a place like Shieldaig, but then it becomes very attractive to observe and maybe for a short time feel part of a lifestyle that on one level isn't very different to the one back home, but on another is a world away. I'd met Karen in my early twenties when we both worked briefly for a firm of accountants, a job that we were probably competent enough at without it suiting either of us for a career. Letting go of her stake in the housing market she had funded herself to take a second degree in biology, then she came to the Shieldaig area ten years or more ago to work in things fish-related. She lived to start with in a wooden cabin before eventually getting lodgings in the schoolhouse, where the sole teacher lives next door to the schoolroom. I suspect two kinds of people move to villages like Shieldaig. One comes for the scenery or to escape from town life, remains aloof, and eventually moves out when the surroundings cease to entertain or there is one harsh winter too many. The other gets involved in village life with its rewards and its frustrations, becomes accepted as part of the community, and begins to see the place as home. Karen much to her credit is definitely the latter sort.

I started to wait for her by the lochside but I was defeated by that scourge of the western Highlands, the midge. Before I scratched myself raw or jumped in the water in desperation I beat a retreat to the inside of the pub, where I had time for half a pint before Karen appeared with her dog Patsy. I ferried them over to *Indalo* in the dinghy and we settled down to a meal of chicken and vegetables with pasta while Patsy made do with ship's biscuits in the cockpit.

On my walk around the village I'd noticed a second, rather basic-looking shop that had once been the main village store. Seeing my Para Handy book on the shelf, Karen mentioned that the shopkeeper, a lady in her seventies, could remember when there wasn't a proper road into Shieldaig and her stock was delivered to the loch-side by puffer. A great number of these little steamships plied the Clyde area and the west coast from the 1880s onwards, gradually replacing their sail-powered equivalents. They were the delivery wagons for the remote communities on the western seaboard, transporting coal, timber, building materials, livestock, general provisions for the villages and barley for the distilleries as well as carrying out operations like dredging. The design of the puffer was dictated by the need to carry a worthwhile load (the smallest took a hundred tons), use drying harbours or even beaches, and unload with its own crane rather than relying on there being one on the quayside. Puffers, many converted to diesel, continued to work on the west coast until the beginning of the 1960s. There are still a few afloat including the diesel-engined *Eilean Esdeal* which runs trips out of Inveraray, and a steam-powered example that was built as a naval supply vessel.

I awoke at Shieldaig at six o'clock on Friday 1st July to a weather forecast predicting strong winds in the afternoon and gales over the weekend. I still had time to get up to Gairloch, a mere sixteen miles away, before the weather front came in. There's a walk-ashore pontoon in the main harbour as well as various boltholes in different parts of the loch, so it made more sense to weather the gale there than at Shieldaig. I raised the mainsail on the anchorage, motored out from behind the island, then shut the engine off and sailed out of Loch Torridon on a gentle southerly breeze. There was no hurry so I drifted slowly up the coast, enjoying the views of sandy beaches backed by low hills in the foreground and bigger mountains in the distance. I identified Port Henderson at the mouth of Loch Gairloch, turned again to the east and motorsailed across the loch to an island called Horrisdale. Tucked in behind it is the sheltered natural harbour of Badachro. This place, I thought, would be a good place to sit out the storm, for though the wind might find its way in it wouldn't raise much of a sea. There were plenty of mooring buoys including some for visitors, as well as a fair scattering of rocks to avoid. Making a mental note of the pilotage I retraced my steps and motored over to the main harbour in Flowerdale Bay to tie up to the pontoon.

The area immediately around Gairloch's little harbour is fairly workaday, but beyond that the setting is rather attractive with beaches of shingle and sand backed by tall hills. The village has a small fishing fleet and a fish marketing business as well as a couple of passenger boats that do whale-watching trips. There are a few shops around and about, though in the immediate vicinity it's easier to buy art and gifts than general provisions. At the head of the bay there's a bridge, an art gallery and the Old Inn. I was in need of refreshment, and as I approached the pub I realised I'd sat outside it a few years back with Karen overlooking the stream that flows into the loch. Inside, the inn is divided into several cosy rooms including a hall with easy chairs around a fireplace, and from what I remembered it not only does good food but decent beer too.

The Old Inn is one of only a few Highland pubs to make it into the Good Beer Guide. I sat in one of the bars and asked for a glass of Blind Piper, mainly so I'd have an excuse to look up the story behind the name. The Blind Piper of Gairloch was Iain or John Dall Mackay, piper to the Mackenzies, who retired in 1750 and came to live in Badachro. Should a piping procession pass by his house he would stand by the roadside and listen. If the piping didn't come up to his high standards he would cover his ears and the piper would stop playing in deference. After his death the tradition continued, and to be sure of not offending his spirit the procession would always go silent near his house. The beer was good too.

My other purpose in coming to Gairloch was to meet Chris, whose bus would stop off at the Old Inn. He had been delayed getting up to Inverness, but the rest of the transport connected well enough and he arrived at about half-five as expected. As we ate in the inn I broke the news that we would be sitting in port for the next few days, probably on a mooring buoy and possibly without being able to get ashore. Earlier in the day I'd spoken to a local boat owner who related some happenings back in January, when a hurricane passed through damaging buildings, overturning boats and uprooting street furniture. A heavy fishing boat was forced aground and turned on its side, and on the pontoon where *Indalo* was berthed his own boat had all its fenders burst leaving the fibreglass hull to grate until it was worn through. There had already been some strong gusts in the afternoon and the pontoon had become distinctly uncomfortable, so I decided that we'd be better off tied to a mooring buoy.

So we left the pontoon early the next morning, motoring over to Badachro and picking up a buoy owned by the Badachro Inn, free to patrons. There was no sign of a gale yet so we inflated the dinghy and went ashore. According to the Welcome Ashore guide that I'd picked up in Ballycastle there was a shop and a petrol station in Badachro, but we couldn't find either and eventually somebody told us both had closed a decade ago. Lack of amenities apart Badachro was an attractive enough mix of old and modern buildings half-surrounding a shallow bay. It even has a house on a little island of its own, connected to the shore by an odd-looking plastic walkway that floats on pipes at high tide.

The Badachro Inn turned out to be a good find. It had an unpretentious wooden bar and a big conservatory with excellent views, and for a price it did laundry and provided showers. After a welcome and filling meal with some more local beer we were joined by some other sailors called Iain and Penny from a catamaran called *Rainbow Catcher* that was moored in the harbour close by. They were helping organise the Cruising Club's round-Britain rally, a non-competitive event involving ten boats going the same way around as *Indalo* and another thirteen, including *Rainbow Catcher*, going anti-clockwise. They had started from Walton in Essex a little before I had set out from Dartmouth. We swapped stories about ports and anchorages on our respective sides of the country, and I came away considering the Tyne as a possible stopover but with less favourable reports of the berthing arrangements at two of the places I was really looking forward to, Berwick and Whitby.

After our repast and discussions we beat the weather back to the boat, where in anticipation of the coming gale I shackled a heavy-duty chain on to the mooring buoy. The blow still hadn't come in by the evening, but according to the late forecast it was imminent and by half-past two on Sunday morning we were in the grip of a severe gale, a force nine. The wind howled through the rigging, the mooring chain snatched and rattled and the rain came in horizontally from the west, but a quick look around the deck confirmed everything was secure and I could go back to sleep, in mental if not physical peace. The gale was still in full force when we got up and there was nothing much to do other than amuse ourselves on the boat until the wind dropped. By mid-afternoon we were bored enough to risk the dinghy trip ashore. With the help of the outboard we were soon safely at the inn for a shower and a meal, discussing our plans for the next day while the weather became calmer by the minute.

In the morning we moved *Indalo* back to the pontoon at Gairloch to top up on supplies. The area around the loch was one of the few places in the Highlands that escaped the Clearances in the eighteenth and nineteenth centuries, when tenant farmers were forcibly evicted from their land and homes to make way for large-scale sheep production. This infamous period in Scotland's history displaced tens of thousands of people and changed the Highland landscape forever, sweeping away small settlements and scattered cottages and replacing them with the occasional planned village. The local Mackenzie lairds didn't 'clear' their land and the result is that rather than a single village Gairloch is more a community of hamlets and dwellings scattered around the loch-head, between them having the facilities of a small town. So rather than a visit to a village centre for our supplies we found a bank a little way from the harbour, bought petrol further up the road in Auchtercairn, went to the shop in Strath, and ate in a café back in Charlestown. Despite having to carry bags and jerry can it was an enjoyable walk, the day was warm and dry and the sun was out, and on the way back we found an all but deserted sandy beach.

In my original plan I'd intended to sail from Shieldaig across the North Minch to Stornoway on the Isle of Lewis, then back again to Kinlochbervie, the last harbour on the west coast. Now we were that much further north in Gairloch we reconsidered and chose to stay on the mainland side, heading first for the fishing port of Lochinver. Slipping the ropes at two o'clock we sailed across the loch and over the shallows inside Longa island at the northwestern entrance, from there turning to the north on course for our first waypoint, the headland of Rubha Reidh. The breeze dropped once we were out of the loch mouth, but we struggled on under sail for the next hour as the conditions were idyllic and it seemed a pity to break the spell with the noise of the engine. Eventually we slowed to walking pace and I reluctantly turned the key in the starter. To the east the Summer Isles shone in the sun, to the southwest I said farewell to Skye, and to the west the flatter profile of Lewis became visible for the first time.

Occasionally on my travels a landfall, a loch or an island is so different to what I'd expected that it is breathtaking, almost unreal. Coming into St Mary's Harbour in the Isles of Scilly for the first time, trickling into the rocky half-land, half-seascape of Chausey off Normandy, and turning out of Kyle Rhea into Loch Alsh are memories that will always stay with me. The approach to Lochinver was an experience to match, with lower ground and islands in the foreground, mountains and forests behind, and the almost impossibly steep cone of the beehive mountain, Suilven, in the background. To round it off the day ended with the clouds lit up in a brilliant red sunset. We had an early start the next morning, but the setting was so spectacular that we had to finish off with a glass of wine in the cockpit while watching the day fade away to the semi-darkness of the brief northern night.

After perhaps two hours' rest we prepared for our final west coast leg up to Kinlochbervie. It was already light when we set off at 0300, but in contrast to the previous day the weather was overcast, cold and still. The passage was uneventful and our view was restricted by mist to the three headlands of Rubha Coigeach, Stoerhead and Point of Stoer.

Otherwise all we saw were some fishing boats close to the shore and the occasional ghostly ship plying the North Minch. At last we turned to starboard and headed in to Loch Inchard, a long and narrow fjord between limestone rocks. Kinlochbervie opened up suddenly to port, we followed a pair of leading marks into the unexpectedly industrial-looking harbour, and we secured *Indalo* to the quay.

Kinlochbervie is a small Highland village attached to a large and ostensibly businesslike fishing port. It has been a working harbour from the 1960s and around twenty years ago it was given enough European money to turn it briefly into the third busiest fishing port in Scotland. Nowadays it's working at well below capacity and it looks sad and deserted. When we arrived the only boats in the harbour were a single fishing boat, an ancient trawler used for trips and charter, a few local dinghies and dayboats, and a second visiting yacht that soon moved on. A single vessel arrived during our stay, a Faroese coaster delivering fish feed. The village itself is one of those places that's not immediately inspiring, but it's fairly well-equipped for a small settlement with among other things a surprisingly large school, and I found it growing on me over the course of the day. Once the harbour is out of sight it's also in an extremely attractive setting.

After getting the domestics out of the way we took a walk around the village. A worn sign pointed to the Kinlochbervie Hotel, and as we hadn't come across any other hostelries we decided to investigate, expecting an equally worn old inn. It turned out to be an uninteresting-looking building in 1970s style, but inside the hotel was smart and welcoming and it had a panoramic view across the village. So we stopped for refreshments and admired the view before returning by way of Loch Clash, a more attractive and less developed inlet that lies just to the north of the village and can be used as an anchorage in calm weather instead of tying up in the harbour.

Back on board in this northernmost of west coast ports I looked at my charts for the next day and reflected on the voyage so far. The next two passages would mark a watershed, for once we were around the north coast and through the Pentland Firth I would be over halfway and it would be easier to continue clockwise than to retrace my path back down the western seaboard. This stretch of coast is the most sparsely-populated in Britain, a coastline of extremes, and I had a strange feeling of heading out of civilisation and entering the far North, a remote, silent, beautiful and perilous wilderness. The chart spoke of tall cliffs and quiet sandy beaches, of desolation and grandeur, of occasional anchorages and harbours too small for *Indalo* to find refuge in, and of tiny, scattered settlements. Contemplating tomorrow's passage around Cape Wrath and on to Scrabster I felt a subdued, reverent excitement.

Wednesday 6th July, day 55 of the voyage, started cool and calm with a light drizzle. We slipped our mooring at 0400 leaving Loch Inchard behind in a panorama of deep blue sea and sky and steely grey cliffs. An hour or so into our passage a dolphin joined us for a few moments to play at *Indalo*'s bow, then we passed outside a tall rock with Cape Wrath now clearly in view. This most isolated of Scottish headlands is rugged and dramatic, a little like a taller, remoter version of the Lizard. Its name is apt for a point exposed to the full fury of the Atlantic, but it's actually and just as appropriately derived from the old Norse for a turning-point. Our own turn we made just over a mile off the Cape to avoid some rocks that lie to its northeast, immediately running into choppy water just as Chris went below to boil the kettle. It wasn't rough enough though to spoil our enjoyment of rounding the Cape and just beyond it the great cliffs of Clo Mòr, at 275m the tallest sea-cliffs in Britain.

From Clo Mòr I set a course eastwards along the coast to clear Faraid Head and distant Whiten Head, while behind us we watched our first fellow vessel of the morning, a yacht on a heading for Shetland. The Kyle of Durness opened up to the south followed a little further on by the eight-mile long Loch Eriboll. Helped by an increasingly strong tide we were soon approaching our lunch stop, the small harbour of Talmine at the entrance to the next great inlet, the Kyle of Tongue. We trickled in slowly, lacking a large-scale chart but aware from the pilot book that there are several rocks in the entrance. Finding a likely spot just clear of some local boats we dropped the anchor. Talmine is a surprisingly homely and sheltered harbour on this most exposed of coasts, with several boats moored to their buoys and a fair few houses scattered here and there behind the bay. Having put over half of the seventy-mile passage to Scrabster behind us and reached the halfway point of the voyage, we settled down for a hot lunch and a siesta while the tide turned against us.

Setting off again at four in the afternoon we motored across the mouth of the Kyle of Tongue and past the improbably sloping little island of Eilean nan Ròn, Isle of Seals, where a crabber was inspecting pots in some sea-caves and three people in an open boat were rolling uncomfortably in the swell. We set a course to clear the next obstacle, Strathy Point, and just as we were drawing level with it Chris spotted what he thought was an orca or killer whale off to starboard. I turned to look and maybe two or three hundred yards away a black-and-white shape lifted out of the sea, stood on its tail and fell back into the water. A couple of minutes later two of the creatures barrelled powerfully past, one streaking below while the other briefly rode our bow wave. Probably females, they nevertheless looked big and fearsome enough at about two-thirds of the length of the boat. *Indalo* wasn't edible and we didn't have any food for them, so they soon lost interest and went off to encircle a shoal of fish.

After Strathy the coast recedes again and the most obvious landmark is Dounreay nuclear plant, a cluster of white buildings with a conspicuous dome simply marked on the chart as 'SPHERE.' A little way further on the cliffs return and run east to Holborn Head, where Thurso Bay opens out with Dunnet Head visible on its far side. Now assisted by two knots of tide we closed with the cliffs, rounded Holborn Head, dropped the mainsail and motored past the ferry quays into Scrabster. The harbourmaster drove around to our side of the quay and directed us into a berth in the port's Inner Basin, then someone from the yacht club called by to tell us where the showers were and see if we needed any assistance. We were in: the longest part of the north coast, if not the most challenging, was behind us.

Scrabster is a bit of a one-horse town with a single restaurant and bar, a small sailing club, no shops and not much else other than the Fishermen's Mission and a harbour-side industrial estate dominated by the BP gas terminal. It's now the main commercial port on the north coast of Scotland, having taken over from the less accessible town of Thurso. A mixture of fishing, ferry traffic to Orkney and the Faeroes, occasional merchant vessels, the odd trip boat, and a few yachts all seem to coexist harmoniously enough. The harbour-master was keen to encourage visitors and he was pleased that twenty yachts had passed through in June, several of them from the Cruising Club's organised circumnavigation. I liked Scrabster's busy, practical and friendly air, and *Indalo* looked comfortable tied up in the corner of the harbour.

Next morning I called in at the harbourmaster's office to pay my dues, and we sat discussing the passage around the Pentland Firth and where to get the best weather forecast on the internet. Our conversation was interrupted by a radio announcement about a terrorist bombing that had just taken place in London, at once jolting me into another reality. Images of familiar places flashed through my mind and my thoughts turned to friends and colleagues who lived or worked in the capital. I felt outrage at the warped mentality that drives people to murder at random in pursuit of a cause or a protest, and despair at the way we as a society fail to unite properly against it. At the same time I had the more resigned thought that it was inevitable that something like this should happen given the questionable nature of some of our recent foreign policy. The other main news of the day was that London was to host the 2012 Olympics, which should have been a reason to celebrate but somehow hearing the two things together filled me with a sense of gloom and foreboding. Even so as I walked back to the boat I felt strangely disconnected from the events, as if they were half a world away and part of a different life. From up here on this Arctic-facing coast the announcer might as well have been talking about happenings in Madrid or Moscow, or even Mumbai or Melbourne.

Back on board, my Scottish guidebook made neighbouring Thurso sound grim and boring as if its only merit was to be the northernmost town in mainland Britain. I knew I was going to like it already, and even if I didn't I needed some exercise. I climbed up above the harbour and took the coast path above some low cliffs, admiring the views across the bay to Dunnet Head. A couple of miles later I entered the town, which struck me as bustling, attractive and rather smart in a Victorian kind of way. The road led straight into the town centre crossroads where the main shopping and eating street stretched out to the right and left. I bumped into Chris, bought some postcards and spent an hour exploring the central area before calling into Le Bistro for an afternoon snack. Le Bistro wasn't very French, but I was the only customer there and I struck up a conversation with the two women who were in there serving, one around my age and the other a girl young enough to be in her first job. From them I picked up quite a lot about life in Thurso, which while not exactly an entertainment hotspot isn't boring or grim either.

Thurso was originally called Thorsaa, Thor's river, and up until the Treaty of Perth in 1266 it was part of Norse Caithness and came under the rule of the Earls of Orkney. Appropriately it's closer by a few miles to Oslo than to

London. For hundreds of years its mainstays have been farming and fishing, but by the nineteenth century there was also a thriving industry quarrying flagstones and shipping them out from the harbour. This provided the impetus for the town's development and for a new centre to be laid out in a modestly grand style under the guidance of local politician and planner Sir John Sinclair. For many years the community was split between the newly prosperous new town or 'up town' and the old 'down town' or fishermen's quarter by the river, but in the 1950s that began to change when the nearby Dounreay experimental nuclear plant brought in the 'atomics' as its workers became called, who mingled with both sets of residents.

Whatever the downside of having a local nuclear establishment (and radioactive pollution of nearby beaches is one of them), Dounreay provided high-tech employment, boosted the economy, nearly tripled the population to eight thousand, and made Thurso a more cosmopolitan town. Local children studied science and went on to college locally and to university further afield, incomers mingled with locals, and the town's outlook broadened. Dounreay will close sometime in mid-century and it's not clear how Thurso will be affected, though there seems to be some thought going into decommissioning so that it will that maintain local employment. Efforts have also been made to develop tourism, although the town suffers a bit because many visitors see it as the gateway to the Orkneys rather than a destination in itself.

After I left Le Bistro I did some shopping, visited the town museum and its eighth-century Pictish standing stones, and walked down to the riverside. Further upstream Thor's river is an important salmon fishery but down here it's not the most attractive of watercourses, at least at low tide. Down town at the seaward end was full of little terraced dormer cottages with a character that shaded somewhere between twee and neat and rough-edged and down-to-earth. Finally I walked back through the town centre and up to the railway station before heading through the back streets for Scrabster. Though the two places are vastly different in style, size and ambience I couldn't help comparing Thurso with Penzance. Both have the feeling of outposts at the end of the road, both seem remarkably self-sufficient, and both are friendly, Thurso if anything the more so. I'd expected to find a bleak little town with nothing much there, and instead it was an attractive and welcoming community that I was sorry only to have spent an afternoon in.

7

Across the Moray Firth

To get from Scrabster to the Scottish east coast without
negotiating the Orkney Islands involves a passage through
the notorious Pentland Firth, potentially the most dangerous
stretch of navigable water anywhere on the British seaboard.
Currents reach up to fourteen knots on spring tides and there
are three tidal races where mountainous seas can build up.

Rocks and shallows lie off the coast to catch the unwary, and steep waves called Pentland Walls can drop ships bow-first into the water. In storm conditions the spray has reached the windows of the Dunnet Head lighthouse a hundred metres above the level of the resting sea. This short stretch of water is Britain's Cape Horn. It's hardly surprising that some ships choose to pass around the Orkneys to avoid it.

Our departure from Scrabster needed to be timed to within half an hour to have the tide with us all the way to Wick, so we left an hour after high water at 0545 to be swept along by the stream. At first the sea was disturbed by only a light swell as we set a northeasterly course across the bay towards Dunnet Head, a trio of great skuas following in our wake. Greedy-looking birds like big seagulls still sporting their brown juvenile plumage, they pestered us until they realised we weren't fishing and weren't inclined to share our breakfast with them. Leaving the skuas in Thurso Bay I steered *Indalo* within half a mile of the headland to admire the cliffs. Dunnet is a massive, pleasingly rounded promontory topped by a stumpy white lighthouse marking mainland Britain's northernmost point. I checked the GPS display as the lighthouse came abeam and logged the most northerly point of the voyage at 58° 40′.8 N, then set the autopilot to steer just south of east to pass the Men of Mey Rocks. North of the rocks the tidal race called the Merry Men of Mey plays merry havoc in the right conditions, but today the Merry Men were sleeping it off and couldn't raise so much as a jig.

Past the Men of Mey we fought a cross-tide to pass between the mainland and the little island of Stroma that forms a sort of halfway house between the Orkneys and Caithness. Before long the tide came back in our favour and we were swept along past the hamlets of Huna and John O'Groats over to starboard. Clearing Stroma I changed course again to take us offshore and out of the influence of Duncansby Race, the final hazard before we could turn south for the run in to Wick. But the race was cancelled so I cut the corner and motored in close to Duncansby Head, the northeastern corner of Scotland, in a sea that was little more than rippled.

The twelve miles from Duncansby south to Wick disappeared in short order as we caught the full flood down the coast, whisking us past tall cliffs and sea-stacks and on to the broad opening that leads into the harbour mouth. Turning into port we made a careful entrance past Robert Stevenson's ruined and sunken breakwater, trickled into the Outer Harbour and tied up next to a redundant ice-plant. After removing several layers of clothing we called into the port office, a charmingly old-fashioned place with a wood-and-glass partition like a 1950s bank or town hall. In the visitors' book I saw that we had missed another Dartmouth boat, *Nefertiti of St Helier*, by a day: bound for Peterhead his entry said. We paid our dues then went our separate ways to explore the town.

Like Thurso Wick is a former Norse settlement; in fact the name (originally Vik, pronounced *week*) just means a bay or inlet, and it comes from the same root as the word Viking, a bay- or fjord-dweller. It's hard to believe now but Wick was once one of the most important fishing ports in Europe. Herring fishing started from the town in the mid-eighteenth century, and by the time the harbour was built in 1822 over eight hundred boats were stationed there, providing work for four thousand people. In the town museum there's a picture of the harbour in 1865, so packed with boats – over a thousand of them – that it was possible to walk from one quay to the other across their decks. This thriving industry brought with it a need for curers, smokers and coopers, and not least for liquid refreshment. At the height of the herring boom a hundred gallons of whisky were consumed in Wick daily and the town had forty-seven inns. But it couldn't last. The herring population declined in the 1930s and the gradually dwindling fleet turned to white fish and shellfish to keep it in business for another fifty years. Today the fishing boats hardly run into double figures, the modern fish market is closed, and the town is one of the most depressed places in Scotland, visible evidence of the ecological and economic tragedy of overfishing.

Wick had a grimness that I couldn't find in Thurso, and there were boarded-up houses and shops and obvious evidence of unemployment and poverty. Having said that it's not as unattractive as it might sound. The river runs through the centre of a pleasing townscape, there's a good selection of shops, and the town boasts some decent places to eat. There also seems to be a fair range of civic amenities including college, hospital, leisure centre and railway station, and my quick impression was that people were friendly and willing to help. There's a feeling of time standing still in parts of Wick; apart from the harbour office some of the shop fronts could have gone unchanged for decades, and there's a similar feel about much of the housing stock as if double-glazing and conservatories had never been in fashion.

After strolling around the town and the harbour area I followed the signs to the Wick Heritage Museum. This excellent and rather cosy museum is run by the Wick Society and staffed completely by volunteers. It's in a terrace of small houses that have been knocked together, and it's completely fascinating. Part of the old harbour is recreated in one gallery and the inside of a lighthouse in another, there's a smokery and a cooper's workshop, as well as a photographic collection from a studio run by three generations of photographers over a period of more than a hundred years. One set of rooms is modelled as the interior of a house from the early part of the twentieth century, some of the oddments and pieces of furniture recalling things I remember from my grandparents' homes. Finally and a little sadly given the state of employment in Wick there's a collection of Caithness glass that had been donated by the factory before it closed.

I found Chris installed outside a pub back in the town centre and joined him for a drink before we adjourned to an Indian restaurant, unprepossessing but good, for dinner. Over our meal we discussed plans for the next few days. I liked Wick but neither of us particularly wanted to stay for a second day. On the other hand Chris wasn't due to fly back from Inverness until Thursday, nearly a week away, and the last sensible point for him to leave from would be Whitehills or Banff, on the south side of the Moray Firth and no more than a fifty-mile sail away. We didn't want to spend our time making ten-mile hops, but nor did we want to cross the Firth all in one go. To compromise we sketched out a nicely symmetrical itinerary with a coastal passage this side of the Firth, a short crossing, and then another passage eastwards to finish in Whitehills. I wanted to call into Latheronwheel purely because of its improbable name (it's actually from the Gaelic for a resort of seals and it's also known as Janetstown), but more sensibly we made Helmsdale our next stop.

Setting out at half-past eight on Saturday morning we would make use of the southwesterly stream to arrive around high water when the sandbanks on the way in to Helmsdale harbour would be submerged out of harm's way. The first part of the passage took us down to Clyth Ness and revealed a coastline of rolling hills gradually giving way to steeper cliffs and sea-caves. To seaward we spotted two large ships, only to realise as their aspect changed that they didn't look very ship-shaped and they weren't moving. I'd seen them on the chart but dismissed them because they were too far out to sea to bother us: they were the twin platforms of the Beatrice oilfield, a small seam in the Moray Firth tapped in the early 1980s and about to become the site of the world's first deep-water wind farm. To starboard the Wick lifeboat passed by at speed, and a few moments later a family in an open motor-dory batted out of one of the sea-caves to greet us.

A little further on the entrance to Helmsdale opened up, I spoke to the harbourmaster on the radio, and we made an entry and tied up to the pontoon. The scene looked inviting and the setting was a bit reminiscent of one of the Glens of Antrim with the river, also called the Helmsdale, cutting its way through the valley and under a picturesque old bridge with a clock tower. Unfortunately there's a newer bridge between the harbour and the original Thomas Telford one to spoil the view, but it does reduce the traffic congestion and as I found out later it makes a good viewing platform. The harbour itself is relatively modern and uses a lot of concrete, but nonetheless it's compact and visually pleasing. Somewhat unusually for a river-harbour it's set off to one side of the river itself, so it's spared from the flow of water coming through and from the silt as well. The original nineteenth-century harbour is just upriver between the two bridges, unused and full of mud.

Once safely berthed we each took brief excursions ashore for shopping, showers and to look around, both coming back willing to take advantage of Highland Harbours' offer of two nights for the price of one. If nothing else there was a smart-looking museum to visit and the promise of some good coastal walks, and I also needed to change *Indalo*'s engine oil. As it happened we were passing the museum on our way to eat when we noticed that the doors were open for an event. Of all the things to do in Helmsdale on a Saturday night we were drawn into an evening of classical North Indian music. At first it sounded little more than the background music in an Indian restaurant, but after a while I realised there was a cyclic rhythm through which it was continually developing and changing and I gradually became drawn into it and lost some of my hunger for a curry.

Next day we had a proper look around the town museum. Housed in an attractive building with an airy modern interior and neat cottage garden outside, it told of Helmsdale's geology and past history. The modern village was laid out by the Duke of Sutherland in the early nineteenth century to accommodate the tenants that he had evicted from his land during the Clearances. Helmsdale became a thriving herring port for a while, but now the fleet's down to eight boats, all crabbers and shrimpers. Nowadays there's hope that tourism will support the local economy: it's an undeniably attractive village or small town with several hotels and guest houses, the river is one of the best for salmon, and there's a small but steady stream of visiting yachts.

Of the many stories told in the museum two that caught my eye were Helmsdale's gold rush and the fate of the last wolf in Scotland. The gold rush started in 1869 when a Sutherland man who had just returned from prospecting in Australia decided to try his luck in the local streams. After getting permission from the Duke it didn't take him long to find gold in Kildonan Burn. The Duke decided to capitalise on the discovery and issued licences for £1 plus ten percent of the take of gold. But by the following year the prospectors were causing enough of a disturbance for him to change his mind and have them cleared off his land. The current landowner is more hospitable and even hires out equipment for those who feel inclined to try their luck.

The wolf story is one of several from different parts of Scotland that lay claim to the country's last wolf. This one is from the year 1700, when a hunter called Polson set out with two young boys who had seen a she-wolf with her cubs in the hills above Helmsdale. They found a cave that looked as if it might be a wolf's lair, and the boys went in to explore. They soon found the cubs, but just at that moment the mother returned and trapped them in the cave. Polson didn't have time to reach his gun, so he caught hold of the wolf and dragged it out of the entrance. After a fierce scuffle he found his knife and stabbed it fatally. What happened to the cubs isn't recorded.

After leaving the museum I took a walk along the coast and back through the countryside, stopping off on the return route to risk a draught Guinness in one of the local hotels. I knew I was on dangerous ground as Helmsdale is about three hundred nautical miles north of Dublin, but I was still non-plussed when the barman managed to pour a pint of the black stuff without a head. It could have been worse: I could have been in the Shetlands.

After a hot and humid night we awoke to a hotter Monday morning, eventually setting out across the firth at noon on a gentle, sparkling sea. The passage began sultry, windless and uneventful. A breeze soon started to stir, and within another half an hour we were making five knots under sail, a welcome change after days of listening to the motor plodding away. Nevertheless the wind direction wouldn't let us make a straight line for our intended destination of Lossiemouth so we needed to tack back and forth. After a couple of hours the breeze dropped and with it the speed, giving us an estimated time of arrival around midnight. With ten miles to go I gave up and started the engine.

Lossie as it's called looked inviting from seaward, a mound of buildings climbing up a low hill punctuated by a church spire and bordered to the left by a broad, dune-backed beach. We arrived slightly after six just as two air force jets screeched overhead, then followed our instructions on to the pontoon at Pitgaveny Quay where we were met by the overall-clad and bicycle-mounted harbourmaster. He welcomed us to Lossiemouth and provided us with a small information pack and the key to the marina and its facilities block. Our pack thoughtfully included a street map that revealed the town to have a formal, grid-pattern layout. We wanted some milk, a drink and a meal, so we headed for what we thought was the town centre – High Street, Queen Street, Prince's Street and so forth – only to find few shops and even fewer places to eat. In the pack was a brochure for a restaurant and bistro, so we headed there and sat outside among the beach crowd drinking lager and eating pizza.

It didn't take long to work out that Lossiemouth was a holiday resort, an RAF base, and at least in part a new town or planned settlement. Our first impressions beyond the harbour area were ambivalent, but as I explored it the place began to grow on me. The planned centre did have a sort of charm and there was a second grid-pattern residential area to the south that had individually-styled bungalows, no pavements and unmade streets, giving it a slightly exotic feel. It all began at the end of the seventeenth century when the nearby town of Elgin wanted a harbour at the mouth of the river Lossie. Two villages grew up, Stotfield on the coast and Seatown on the river, eventually connected in the 1830s when local landowner James Brander laid out the streets of what was then called Branderburgh in the middle. Riding on the herring boom Brander also built the present harbour, which remained a trading port for a hundred years while also attracting a respectable fishing fleet. The other fact about Lossie that doesn't take too much searching out is that it was the birthplace in 1866 of James Ramsay Macdonald, in the 1920s the first Labour prime minister.

As the tide didn't become favourable for our passage east until mid-afternoon we could continue our exploration the following morning. Pitgaveny Quay has a rather attractive row of shops, bars and converted warehouses with a broad quayside and a row of yachts below, now bathed in the morning sun. One of the warehouses is now the local museum, housing some model ships, yachts and fishing boats as well as a mock-up of Ramsay Macdonald's study. It wasn't particularly revealing about the town's history but it did explain why Lossie fishermen are spared working on Christmas day: in the Stotfield disaster of Christmas 1806 a sudden southwesterly gale swept the fleet out to sea, drowning 21 men and boys. Outside I had a look at some of the other yachts and paid a visit to the harbourmaster, now in smart captain's uniform, to settle up for the harbour dues. Finally we patronised one of the other warehouses where they were serving light lunches, and sat outside on the quay basking in the fierce midday sun.

Leaving Lossiemouth at half-past two we motored due east for Whitehills with not a sign of the light westerly wind that the forecast promised. Just over halfway a moderate northeasterly began to blow instead, but it left us enough of an angle to sail down the coast and almost straight into our destination. Outside the harbour we played with heaving-to, backing the foresail to work against the mainsail and hold the boat roughly still in the water. From our hove-to position I called the harbour on both the VHF channels given in my pilot book and a different one from the Welcome Ashore guide, and I tried the telephone number, but all to no avail. So we dropped the sails and carefully entered the narrow dogleg at the mouth of Whitehills, crept into the tiny, packed inner harbour, couldn't see anywhere to berth, and decided to go out again and tie up to a pontoon in the outer basin. As I was about to swing *Indalo's* bow around to make an exit she was caught by a gust of wind and hit the harbour wall before crabbing sideways back out through the narrow entrance, a couple of feet to spare fore and aft. Fortunately nothing was coming the other way and we tied her up safely, eventually encountering the harbourmaster and discovering which channel we should have been calling him on.

In the morning we moved *Indalo* into the inner harbour and went a walk around the village, which turned out to be rather pleasant if not the most exciting place on the Moray Firth. The harbour was built about a hundred years ago for fishing boats and it's well-protected with sturdy walls. A few years back resident yachts began to outnumber the fishermen and pontoons were put in to the inner section. It's exceptionally friendly, well-run and welcoming, the facilities are good and there's even a visitors' kitchen-cum-lounge. My only criticism is that they have tried to cram in too many boats, though once you know how things work there seems to be no shortage of people willing to take ropes and help tie up.

Later on we met up with a retired engineer from Wells in Norfolk who had berthed his big Southerly yacht a couple of pontoons away from *Indalo*. We headed off to the village pub where we were joined by the large and hungry crew of a boat called *Julia*. Fellow circumnavigators, the owners had set out anti-clockwise from the west coast of Scotland. Running out of time in the English Channel they hired a professional skipper and crew so they could push on: from the Channel to Lowestoft, Lowestoft to Peterhead in one go, and now to Whitehills where the crew were about to depart, leaving the owners to carry on to Inbhir Nis and through the Caledonian Canal. We had a good evening over a hearty meal and a few pints discussing our respective experiences, and I went away with a good report of Peterhead or at least its marina.

On Thursday Chris caught the bus to Inverness while I set out in the drizzle to walk to Banff, two or three miles up the coast. Just out of Whitehills there was a board with some information on it about the local area. One of the things it pointed out was a domed shelter-like building a hundred yards or so away, housing the Red Well. Originally made by the Romans, it was supposed to have medicinal properties and once formed an essential part of any itinerary around Banffshire. It's now marked 'unfit for human consumption.' I wondered if it had become polluted by nitrate run-off or some other act of human negligence, or whether it was just that yesterday's medicine had become today's poison. I hadn't realised that the Romans had built anything so far north, even less that they used metric measurements (for the building is exactly three metres to the top of the ceiling and the door is one metre by two). Apparently they might also have used it as a calendar of sorts because on the autumn and spring equinox the rising sun illuminates the interior of the little building before anything else.

The information board also told the story of a young maid whose employer, the local laird, had forced himself on her. Ashamed and not knowing whom to turn to, she fled the house and sat on the shore in her cloak and wept. But it was a cold night, and she died from exposure. Saddened, I walked across the beach and past a terrace of rather twee sea-front cottages, emerging in Banff by its old harbour. There were a few small yachts and motorboats there, but it was low tide and the thick soft mud around the edges made the place look down-at-heel. I wandered into the town, found the bus stop in case I needed it later, then discovered the rather neat Barclays Hotel and treated myself to a hearty lunch. Like Whitehills I wasn't exactly excited by Banff, but it wasn't a bad place either. Some parts still reflected its days as an elegant Georgian resort, while others looked as if they had seen better times.

Next stop was Macduff, separated from Banff by a few hundred yards and the River Deveron, which is crossed by an arched road bridge built by John Smeaton of Eddystone Lighthouse fame. Macduff is more of a working town than Banff, and as well as housing the first decent fishing fleet I'd seen since Ardglass it's also a base for building and repairing fishing boats and the last place in Britain where you can order a full-sized trawler made of wood. Next to its busy harbour an attractively old-fashioned double-fronted shop serves as a fish wholesaler, chandler and the harbourmaster's office. I went in and bought some small items of chandlery, mostly just for the pleasure of buying something there.

Just past the harbour area is Macduff's excellent marine aquarium. This gem is housed in a purpose-made circular building that has several rooms each containing a different marine habitat. When I went in a loudly-spoken Geordie girl was feeding some of the fish and explaining to a gaggle of children what and how they eat ("yes, your fingers if you put them there"). The *piece de resistance* and literal centrepiece of the aquarium is a deep-water kelp-reef habitat that occupies a tall cylindrical tank in the middle of the building. It's viewed from a cinema-style gallery where the tank appears like a screen. I'd seen the same sort of thing on a bigger scale in

Plymouth and Sydney, but this one was almost more interesting because it was full of species that were familiar from the fishmonger's slab: cod, saithe or coley, haddock, pollack and sole, as well as the odd lobster and an evil-looking wolf fish, a sort of deep-sea catfish that's normally skinned and sold like many other denizens of the deep as rock salmon. The only thing lacking was a tea room.

Friday was my day of departure for Peterhead. According to both the pilot book and the Admiralty tidal atlas of the North Sea I would need to set out at about 1345, stem a weak tide for three hours or so, then carry the tide the rest of the way to the Blue Toon as it's called for an arrival at about ten in the evening. From what I'd seen of tides along this coast I suspected that the information wasn't quite right, and the harbourmaster's advice was to leave a couple of hours earlier near local low water.

Following the local knowledge I'd acquired I slipped my mooring just before mid-day, carefully made my way off-shore, and once clear of the rocks I hauled the mainsail up in a rolling sea before turning east. The wind was moderate and from the northwest so I was able to make a respectable pace under sail. I set the windvane but the swell kept trying to spin *Indalo* around to windward before the vane pulled her back on course, producing a neat serpentine pattern on the GPS screen. Fed up with my corkscrew progress and afraid I'd be caught out by an accidental gybe I went back to manual steering. Banff and Macduff passed by in short order, followed by the village of Gardenstown looking from seaward like a row of beach huts. Now I had the tide with me and before long the lighthouse on Kinnaird Head in Fraserburgh became visible in the distance. Next came Rosehearty and Sandhaven, little drying harbours, and a little while later I came abreast of the Broch itself.

Before setting out I'd toyed with calling into Fraserburgh and visiting the Northern Lighthouse Board's museum, but as the town's a busy fishing port without any facilities for yachts I'd decided to give it a miss. The wind dropped as if to persuade me to change my mind, but I put the engine on and set a course across the submerged Steratan shelf north of Inverallochy to come within a mile of Rattray lighthouse. Rattray Head marks the corner of the eastern bulge of Scot-land and it's got a reputation for raising a rough sea in bad weather: in poor conditions it's sensible to stand off by as much as five miles. Today it was fairly calm, and apart from the offshore lighthouse Rattray looked anything other than a major tidal headland. It's basically a series of sand-dunes with greenery on top, backed by an oil- or gasworks: none of the high drama of Cape Wrath, Dunnet or the Lizard. Nevertheless the tide picked up to two and a half knots around the headland and the wind returned, so it wasn't long before I was closing on Peterhead and its great harbour.

Being a busy commercial port the Blue Toon requires vessels to radio ahead and get permission to enter. I duly called up port control and was told to proceed, chased in by a merchant ship that was doing its best to catch me up. Inside the breakwaters the fishing boats have their own harbour off to the right, oil and gas support vessels berth to the left, and the marina is straight on. As soon as I'd tied up I went below to check the log. I'd travelled 39 miles over the ground but only 34.5 through the water, the tide doing the rest. The harbourmaster at Whitehills had given me good advice and the pilot book and Admiralty tidal atlas had been misleading. The atlas can be excused because the research it's based on was done for big ships and it doesn't show inshore currents, but the yachting pilot should have been more informative.

Peterhead marina is on a bigger scale than anything I'd encountered since leaving Ireland. The pontoons are well-spaced so it's easy to manoeuvre, and the facilities are good. The drawback is that it's situated about a mile from the town and there are no pubs or eating-places any closer: reversing the usual trend the nearest one had not long ago been turned into a church. So I set out along the sea front towards the town and headed for the much-recommended Palace Hotel with its American-themed, Oriental-staffed restaurant.

Next morning I was due to meet Carmeen, an old friend from student days. Since leaving university she had married and returned to her native Northern Ireland, then ten or twelve years ago she moved with her family across to Scotland, settling in Banchory to the west of Aberdeen. She was slightly delayed which was just as well because the showers had been commandeered by the sizeable crew of the *Atene,* a Swedish sail training ship, and my ablutions had to wait until mid-morning. Carmeen arrived a little before midday with teenagers Alex and Suzanne but minus husband Howard who was out playing golf. We had a chat on board, the youngsters inspected the boat, then we went to the Palace for lunch and took a drive into the country to see the Pitfour Observatory. A light-coloured stone tower, it was built in 1845 for Admiral George Ferguson to provide a grandstand view over his private racecourse. It's also supposed to have good views across Buchan or wherever it was we were, but by the time we had got there and tramped up the path to the tower the weather had turned to fine drizzle and all we could see were the surrounding woods and fields.

Back at the harbour we called in to the smart modern maritime centre that stands next to the beach just townward of the marina. I was aware of the town's importance as a fishing port and its more recent role as a base for support vessels for the offshore oil and gas industries, but I didn't know that it once had Britain's biggest whaling fleet, in the mid-nineteenth century amounting to 31 ships. Then rather predictably came herring, and then white fish. Peterhead still has a sizeable offshore fleet and claims to be Europe's leading white fish port, though it's apparent that fishing is no longer the source of wealth that it once was. The other thing I learned was that the harbour had had a visit from John Smeaton, who built the outer breakwaters with labour from the local prison.

The centre was also playing host to the Boaties Summer Residency. Boaties are model Fifies, the traditional fishing boats of north-east Scotland. The residency involves boatie-makers passing on their skills to apprentices, generally local teenagers with less than advantaged backgrounds. There were boaties in various stages of construction as well as a few finished articles, and the craftsmen and apprentices were keen to share their enthusiasm for what they were doing. A boatie takes around six weeks to make, the materials and methods mirroring those used for real Fifies. The finished craft would be raced at a local regatta in a fortnight's time.

Carmeen said farewell over tea and cakes and we made plans to meet up in a few days after I'd moved further south. I'd wanted to berth in Aberdeen, but I wasn't sure that the city would welcome *Indalo* because it's a major oil and gas port and it doesn't really encourage yachts, more because of the problem of getting them in and out among the constant stream of support vessels than through any lack of space. The almanac and pilot book weren't very complimentary and they suggest that the berthing fees are designed to discourage visitors, but I rang the port office and they couldn't have been more helpful. "No problem, seventeen pounds for up to five nights, we'll put you on the old ferry pontoon and you can use the shower in the fish market." Not the luxury of Peterhead marina, but it didn't sound a bad deal for a berth in the heart of the city particularly if I stayed for more than one night. I made some pilotage notes for entering the harbour, finished reading my Para Handy book, and went to sleep.

According to local wisdom the best time to leave Peterhead for a passage south is about low water, a full three hours before the tidal stream turns offshore. This would mean around four in the afternoon, so I decided to use the morning to do the Peterhead town trail as advertised on a leaflet in the marina. It's a fairly short route around the fish harbour, town centre and fishermen's quarter so I judged I'd have plenty of time to wander up to the town, do the walk, have lunch and stroll back. The fishing harbour up in the northeastern corner of the *avant port* was the town's original harbour and dates from the sixteenth century, though the current breakwaters are about two hundred years old. There were some impressively large offshore trawlers in port, the kind that can go to sea for weeks at a time, as well as an ultra-modern fish market that appears to be thriving unlike its counterpart in Wick. Right next to the road was one of the old-style dry docks with stepped sides to make it easier to work on the ship's hull. The other interesting area was the fishermen's quarter, a back street called Roanheads where the fishermen used to live two or three centuries ago. Unfortunately the neat little cottages soon gave way to modern flats with 'no ball games' signs, identical to the ones in Penzance.

Otherwise I thought Peterhead was pretty drab. It isn't doing too badly with the gas and oil industries and there's still enough fishing and fish landing to keep things going, but somehow the town managed to seem a bit dead and slightly scruffy. Partly that might have been because it was a Sunday morning after a summer Saturday night, but in spite of some rather grand buildings and streets the place had a curious down-at-heel feel to it, as if it had once been rather wealthy and it was now embarrassed by the circumstances it found itself in. There's nothing particularly objectionable about Peterhead and I'd berth there again if I ever find myself back on this section of coast, but it's not somewhere I'd go out of my way to visit.

Back at the marina I bumped into Keith from *Dart Dash*, who I'd met in Oban and assumed would be far ahead of me by now. He had taken the short cut through the Caledonian Canal and was intending to stop in Peterhead for a couple of days before heading for Stonehaven. I ribbed him about missing the best bits, made up a story about thirty-foot waves in the Pentland Firth, and went aboard to prepare for the short passage to Aberdeen.

I left the marina as instructed at low water Peterhead, 1545 clock time. As I turned south out of the harbour both wind and tide were against me and I struggled to make four knots over the ground. At least it was warm and sunny. Two hours later there was still half a knot of tide to deal with and the wind was increasing. By seven I cleared the southern end of Cruden Bay and the tide had at last gone slack, though the wind was freshening and the spray scudded over the deck. A dolphin played in my bow-wave and came up to the cockpit to say hello, but he swam off when I offered him a tow-rope so I just opened the throttle and got on my way. The advice I'd been given would have been fine if I'd been heading for Stonehaven or further south, but now I realised that the best tactic for Aberdeen would have been to leave at half-tide up and have the current with me all the way.

At last I drew level with the Aberdeen fairway buoy and called up port control. Go just north of the entrance came the reply, and wait for our call. I dropped the sail and boiled the kettle. A ship departed, the harbourmaster gave me clearance to enter, and I gunned the engine to get in before the next ship was due to leave. Arriving in the Albert Basin I berthed alongside a Dutch-flagged yacht that had done the trip from Peterhead earlier in the day and was taking a break before heading home. Safely ensconced in Aberdeen I had a cup of tea and turned in. The city could wait until tomorrow.

8

Granite City to Walled Burgh

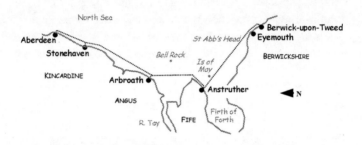

It was Monday 18th July, and I was in Aberdeen, the Granite
City (or Silver City to those who have only seen it in the sun)
of Scotland's north-east. My first stop of the morning was the
Maritime Museum, a spacious modern three-storey affair that
relates the history of Aberdeen as a port and includes lots of
models, mock-ups and technical exhibits on the city's three
main maritime enterprises: the oil industry, shipbuilding and
fishing. There was a good attempt to explain the issue of
dwindling fish stocks and the need for conservation measures, and the arguments of the fishing industry and conserva-
tionists were put forward in a fairly even-handed way. The
storyboard concluded that fishing needs to be reduced if
stocks are to be replenished, hardly surprising given what I'd
seen in almost every Scottish port I had visited. I was though
slightly taken aback to read that around half the bed of the
North Sea is disturbed annually by fishing, in addition to oil
and gas extraction and miscellaneous dumping and pollution.

The museum explained that Aberdeen's maritime history had followed a similar pattern to Peterhead's, first as a whaling harbour, then herring, and finally white fish before its decline as a fishing port in the 1980s. It was also a centre of shipbuilding for much of the twentieth century, though not on the scale of the Clyde, the Wear or the Tyne, and it had to wait until the era of North Sea oil to fully recover its prosperity. From the discovery of the Forties field in 1970 the city became the hub of the British oil industry, boosting its economy and making it as expensive to live in as Edinburgh. The oil boom has undoubtedly done Aberdeen a lot of good, but the high prices and cost of living have put other industries off investing in the city. When the price of oil plummeted in 1986 over four thousand local jobs disappeared in the oil and gas industries followed by half as many again in other parts of the economy. There wasn't much of a problem at the time of my visit (petrol had just gone up to over 90p a litre) but it's easy to see how vulnerable Aberdeen could be.

From the museum I walked across to the tourist office for some information and a map, surprising the woman behind the counter when I told her I'd come into the city in a yacht. Next I went for a stroll down Union Street. This mile-long shopping street is Aberdeen's equivalent of London's Oxford Street or Edinburgh's Prince's Street, and it wouldn't look out of place in either capital. In fact it's smarter than Oxford Street and there's as almost as much variety and a lot less tat. I noted the location of a tapas bar that Carmeen had recommended then I stopped off at a church that had been converted into a pub, more because I was intrigued than in need of a drink. The bar area was dark and snazzy with leather sofas and glass tables, not quite what I'd expected but interesting enough for me to buy half a lager and take in the atmosphere. It wouldn't have been out of place on the other side of the world in Sydney or Melbourne, but it worked in a strange sort of way and it was atmospheric without feeling like being in a church.

135

In the afternoon I decided to explore the old fishermen's and artisans' quarter of Footdee ('Fittie'), have a look at the beach, and finally make my way back into town and to the La Tasca that I'd checked out earlier. The walk from the docks to Footdee is uninspiring and goes through a roughish industrial area. As I was passing a pub I was hailed by a woman dressed in denim who had been hanging around on the corner. She spoke to me in broad Aberdonian Doric which may as well have been Gaelic for all I could understand. I told her I was looking for Fittie which she didn't seem interested in, or maybe my south of England accent was just as unintelligible to her. She could have been soliciting or asking for money or for a light, or just passing the time of day. Just as I wondered if the place existed at all I spotted a high-gabled brick cottage, crossed the road and came into Footdee, a few small terraced squares and streets with little brick outhouses and well-tended front gardens. It's a complete contrast to the grand style of central Aberdeen, and it's rather attractive and intimate. Nevertheless I was disinclined to linger, feeling I was intruding on the privacy of the residents.

From Fittie I walked along the sea front. Aberdeen is also a holiday town of sorts and it has an enviable sandy beach, divided by groynes into a pattern of squares that closer up become little individual beaches. Opposite there's a collection of seaside amusements, a big funfair, and the usual mix of seaside eating places. From the beach a road leads back into town (I cut across the grass) and passes some expensive-looking apartments to arrive at the eastern end of Union Street. So I walked down Union Street again and went into La Tasca. I'd not been into one of these before but the ambience and the food were both good. The downside to sitting alone eating tapas is that it's too tempting to order too many dishes and eat too much and then have a sweet and a coffee, and then a Spanish aperitif and maybe an After-Eight or whatever it is that comes with the liqueur. I waddled down the remainder of Union Street, found a little piece of Edinburgh called Bon Accord Crescent, followed some back streets until they came out by the railway, and finally emerged by the River Dee on a busy main road that took me to the harbour. While I'd been away *Atene* had come in, the Swedish sailing ship that had been in Peterhead. I set my alarm really early for the shower.

On Tuesday I'd arranged to meet Carmeen in the smart little town of Banchory, setting off from the bus station near the docks. The bus follows the Dee valley so I sat up top for the view, but once it was out of Aberdeen it started raining heavily and there wasn't one to speak of. The bus wound its way out of the city, then it passed a sign saying 'Welcome to Aberdeenshire.' I'm not sure how administrative areas and regions work in Scotland, but they seem slightly odd. I don't know why Aberdeen isn't in its shire or why only a few miles further on we stopped being in Aberdeenshire and emerged into Kincardineshire. On the west coast there wasn't much mention of administrative districts apart from Skye and Lochalsh (why is an island lumped in with a bit of the mainland?), but there was occasional reference to topographical areas such as Morvern and Knoydart and regions like Lochaber and Wester Ross. Up north Caithness and Sutherland were easy enough to understand as they had remained unchanged since Norse times, but around the Moray Firth every port seemed to be in a different area or county: Easter Ross, Nairn, Moray, Banffshire (or Banff and Buchan), and so on. To add to the confusion there's a body called the Highland Council that runs the harbours in places as distant as Kyleakin, Kinlochbervie and Helmsdale. It may be the result of all the messing about with local government boundaries that goes on from time to time, or it might just make better sense if you grew up north of the border.

Getting off at Banchory's High Street I walked around the corner into the Pennyfarthing teashop where I met Carmeen. Despite the rain, which was now easing anyway, we decided to take a walk back along the Dee towards Crathes, a small settlement marked out by a castle or tower-house with a rather fine garden. In spite of some noise from chainsaws and brushcutters in the woods the walk was quite pleasant. We might have seen otters fishing or salmon leaping but we didn't, only other people with mountain bikes who were sat by the river. A disused railway line was being restored for use, which I thought was quite commendable until Carmeen said it would only be a short stretch of steam railway from Banchory to Crathes. It would have been nice to report that it was going all the way to Aberdeen and taking some of the pressure off the well-used A96, but it wasn't.

⚓

The rain had gone by the time I got back to Aberdeen and the forecast for Wednesday was predicting a fresh northwesterly increasing to a near-gale later. In the morning the Icelandic source I'd been recommended in Scrabster indicated nothing more than a gentle or moderate breeze at first, freshening in the afternoon and strengthening overnight. I'd half hoped for a sunny day with strong winds so I'd have an excuse to stay put and visit Aberdeen's old town and university, but the weather was for sailing early and sitting tight later. Though I wasn't due to meet Ian, my next crew, until Thursday night there was no harm in spending some time down the coast in Stonehaven. I made up a quick passage plan and prepared to set off.

Slipping the ropes at half-past nine in the morning I left astern of a work-boat, *Atene* having set off ten or fifteen minutes earlier. The breeze was at least moderate so I hoisted sail just outside the harbour entrance and turned to face south. With wind and tide in my favour I was soon storming along the coast, and less than three hours after clearing Aberdeen's breakwaters I dropped the sails ready to enter Stonehaven harbour while *Atene* looked for a place to anchor outside. I tied up next to an unoccupied steel yacht and made a dash for the shower before the Swedish advance guard could get ashore. I needn't have worried: when I looked again they had upped anchor and gone.

Stonehaven is a rather attractive town that serves as harbour, holiday resort and the county town of Kincardineshire. Its natural harbour was extended in stages from the sixteenth century to the beginning of the twentieth, and it now has three distinct parts all with stone breakwaters. Originally coasters brought coal and lime and went away with grain, whisky, potatoes and cured fish, then like almost everywhere on the east coast Stonehaven played host to a herring fleet. Nowadays it's filled with pleasure boats, though there's still a small group of shellfishing vessels that lends a sense of purpose and busyness to the middle quay. There are some old houses and inns along the quayside and the whole scene is rather pleasing.

Later in the afternoon the local dinghies came out in force. I watched the colourful little fleet playing in the evening sun, bigger boats outside the breakwater and children's ones inside. Just as the fleet retired for the evening a boy of about eight or nine managed to collide with *Indalo*'s rudder, tangle himself up with his boat's tiller, and sail sideways into the harbour wall before the rescue boat could get to him. Soon after the dinghies had come in Keith from *Dart Dash* wandered over to the head of the quay and invited me to join him for a pub meal. We sojourned to the Ship Inn on the harbourside to discuss our experiences since leaving Oban and our plans for the journey south. All being well we would sail in company to Arbroath on Friday.

The next day I had lunch in Stonehaven's rather stylish Art Deco Carron restaurant. Afterwards I set off for a walk, working my way through the streets at the back of the harbour until I found a track beside the police station that led uphill to a clifftop viewpoint. The view was well worth the short climb: the three-part harbour, Stonehaven town and the bay were all laid out in front of me. I took some photographs then walked past a sign that said 'Welcome to Stonehaven – birthplace of R W Thomson, inventor of the pneumatic tyre.' Important though the pneumatic tyre is, it seems slightly odd to choose as the town's main claim to fame the fact that its inventor was born there. When was he born, I wondered, and did he stay there long? Did he do his inventing in Stonehaven, or had he migrated to somewhere like Edinburgh, the States or the East Indies? Did he invent anything else, and did he ever return?

A pair of cyclists came around the corner on four of his inventions and disappeared down the hill. I formed a picture of the sort of bikes they might have been riding if it wasn't for R W Thomson, then corrected myself and visualised a contemporary velocipede with twenty-seven gears, ultra-lightweight tubing and of course solid tyres, but flexible, grippy ones rather than the old hard sort. At least they wouldn't go flat. I repaired countless punctures as a teenager, and I wondered if without Mr Thomson's invention some alternative advance would have been made in tyre technology that would have saved me the effort.

Nowadays I'm only an occasional cyclist but I do like a walk, and the least I was going to do was to follow the coast path over to Dunnottar Castle. The path meanders up and down alongside clifftops and across fields with views over rocky inlets white with seabirds. The castle gradually came into view, at first appearing to sit unremarkably on an extension of the fields. Rounding the next small headland it becomes clear just what a good site it's on. The castle sits astride a rocky crag overlooking the sea, almost separated from the mainland; it would be hard to imagine it being taken by force before the age of artillery. Even in the Civil War it held out for eight months against Cromwell's army and won itself a special place in Scotland's history. The country's crown jewels had been taken there for safekeeping, and when the castle eventually fell they were long gone, smuggled out in a fish basket.

Today the castle was being besieged by rival coachloads of French and German tourists, so given that and the advancing hour I beat a retreat and set off to find Dunnottar woods. Several fields and muddy paths later I still hadn't found them, though I did discover another route into Stonehaven that took me past some rather fine late nineteenth century houses to the back of the town and over to the northern end of the bay where there was an open-air swimming pool. Finding a route back to the harbour by way of a beachside boardwalk I cleaned off my muddy footwear and looked in at the Marine Hotel, neighbour of the Ship. Its upstairs restaurant had a charming and slightly out-of-date ambience with bare wooden tables, metal and wicker chairs and an old and rather faded red carpet. It was the type of place that could so easily be renovated or given a facelift, and totally spoiled. I sat at a window with a harbour view and enjoyed the atmosphere and the food, which if not exactly gourmet was more than good enough.

Ian arrived on the quayside late in the evening. Over the afternoon a swell had got up from seaward making *Indalo* pitch and roll uncomfortably, not helped by the fact that our neighbour was tied very loosely to the quay so that her owner could go off and leave her without the bother of adjusting ropes as the tide rose and fell. We retied both sets of ropes as best we could and put all seven of *Indalo's* fenders out, but the effect was at best marginal. After seventy days aboard I could hardly let a bumpy night bother me, but it was a bit of a rude welcome for Ian.

Friday's timetable made for a gentle start, letting us wake up slowly before preparing for the run down to Arbroath. Run it would be, as the wind had moved around towards the northeast and was now moderate to fresh, which should make for fast sailing. *Dart Dash* and another identical Contessa were leaving at the same time, so we would have some company until the bigger boats left us in their wake. We slipped at eleven with the other yacht slightly ahead and *Dart Dash* about five minutes behind. We lost no time in getting the sails up and *Indalo* was soon making five to six knots downwind. The wind changed direction a few times but we kept up a good pace and with it our lead until *Dart Dash* overhauled us off Montrose. The other boat headed offshore to look for more wind, but with little success as we held comfortably on to middle place. Soon after four in the afternoon we dropped sail and motored into Arbroath on the heels of *Dart Dash*, the third yacht about ten minutes adrift. It had been an excellent passage and it made up a bit for Ian's uncomfortable first night: warm and sunny, plenty of wind, and sailing all the way. Not bad going either against two highly-rated cruiser-racers.

Arbroath harbour is quite active fishing-wise as well as attractive in a workaday sort of way, and next to it are the sheds where they turn haddock into the delicious Arbroath smokies. Otherwise my first impression wasn't very favourable, as the town is spoiled by the anonymous main roads that have been built through it bringing a plague of drab concrete and scruffy grass verges. The centre is rather better though and the main shopping street has kept much of its architectural character. Plus of course there are the red-stone ruins of the abbey. Apart from smoked fish the town is famous for the Declaration of Arbroath, Scotland's proclamation of independence, drawn up at the abbey in 1320 six years after Robert the Bruce had defeated Edward II at Bannockburn. The Declaration was a letter from Scotland's barons to the Pope of the day asking him to lift the order of excommunication with which, at the instigation of Edward I, he had tarred all Scots. It's not only a high-minded affirmation of independence that was to inspire the later American version, but like England's Magna Carta it contains the seeds of a constitutional monarchy. Robert, it declared, was king only on condition that he upheld Scotland's independence from England: if he didn't, the barons could dethrone him and find someone else.

Over an evening meal – an Italian as Ian isn't a great piscivore and wasn't desperate to sample the smokies – we discussed the logistics for the next couple of days. Ian hails from Dundee, and my original thoughts had been to part company with him at Broughty Ferry, a small haven in the River Tay within hailing distance of the town. From Arbroath that's hardly a proper sailing passage away, and as he wasn't due to leave until Sunday it would also mean losing a day sitting around in the Tay estuary. What's more the Tay isn't an ideal port of call as the tides are strong in the entrance and they would make it difficult to time a passage going south. Ian reluctantly abandoned the idea of calling in to Dundee to let us push on via Anstruther to somewhere on the other side of the Forth, where he would meet up with his wife ready to go on to a walking holiday in the Highlands.

On Sunday we spent some time exploring the town before having a hearty lunch of pies, Scotch rolls and some bridies, like small Cornish pasties for carnivores. Then it was time to catch the tide for our next passage to Anstruther, or Anster as it's abbreviated locally. The wind had dropped overnight so the sails needed some help from the engine, but the sun was out and we could relax and admire the view with the autopilot doing the steering. We crossed the Tay some distance off, so Broughty Ferry was lost in the haze as Ian looked homeward through the binoculars and I studied the distinctive cigarette-shaped Bell Rock lighthouse off to port.

The light on Bell Rock is the work of Robert Stevenson, Scotland's greatest lighthouse-builder and a worthy successor to John Smeaton. Stevenson was born in 1772 and had as a stepfather the first chief engineer of the Northern Lighthouse Board. At the age of nineteen he had a hand in the light at Little Cumbrae, followed soon after by the one on the Pentland Skerries. Between 1799 and 1811 he worked, initially alongside the engineer John Rennie, on the difficult task of putting a lighthouse on the semi-submerged Bell Rock. For this great feat of engineering Stevenson studied and improved on Smeaton's Eddystone light, establishing his reputation as the leading civil engineer of his age; over the next two decades he produced lights for the Northern Board at the rate of nearly one a year. Like Smeaton he didn't confine himself to lighthouses and his engineering feats included harbours, canals, roads, railways, bridges and monuments. The celebrated box-girder railway bridge over the Menai Strait to Anglesey was his, though it has since been largely replaced after a fire. Less happily his breakwater at Wick didn't withstand the ravages of the sea and it's now no more than a navigational hazard beneath the waves. Robert's sons and grandsons included another five civil engineers as well as the author Robert Louis, and together the family was responsible for nearly a hundred lights around the Scottish and Manx coasts.

Leaving Bell Rock behind we closed with the land at Fife Ness, the point where the Tay estuary gives way to the Forth. Rounding the Ness I brought *Indalo* in close enough to get a good look at Crail, one of Scotland's most photographed and painted harbours. Anstruther is only a short hop down the coast from Crail so a little later we were heading into port. Ian had been there as a child, and from his description I imagined it as a small, quiet fishing harbour backed by a village with a pub and a shop. In fact it was a busy little holiday town caught in the middle of an RNLI fundraising event, complete with high-speed lifeboat trips and bungee-jumping over the water from a crane. Why bungee-jumping I don't know though perhaps it was a good time to be doing it with the lifeboat crew standing by. We tied up and walked ashore for the last of the action as the lifeboat was hauled out and packed away into its house.

We needed to leave Anstruther by six the following morning to avoid being trapped by the falling tide, so we had just enough time for a short walk around the harbour area and a visit to a restaurant before turning in for an early night. Our sleep was disturbed by Saturday night revellers, but we were up in time and escaped from the harbour with half an hour to spare. We left powered by a gentle northeasterly, enough to make way under sail, but it was cold and brought an uncomfortable North Sea swell with it. Making our way across the Firth of Forth we headed just inside the Isle of May, a small lighthouse-bearing island that's a favourite of local trip boats and home to forty thousand puffins, then altered course for the far shore of the Forth and the run down to Berwick-upon-Tweed.

When we came into Anstruther I'd noticed that the echo-sounder wasn't registering properly, and I'd optimistically put it down to the muddy bottom of the harbour. Since leaving in the morning it had stubbornly flashed 3.9 metres regardless of the depth of the sea bed. If I couldn't fix it I wasn't going to chance entering Berwick, as misjudging the depth with an onshore swell could mean being pounded on to the sandbanks at the mouth of the Tweed. I left the steering to Ian and the windvane and went below to sort it out. I unscrewed a wooden panel and checked the wiring, then looked at the physical installation of the sounder beneath the starboard berth. All seemed OK and the swell was starting to make me feel queasy, so I came up. The echosounder still wasn't working properly so Berwick was off the list. I rang Dunbar, but the waves were too big to enter. The other option was Eyemouth, accessible from half-tide up.

By now both wind and boat speed were dropping, the swell had increased, there was a light mist, and it was still chilly. We voted to put the motor on. There was no hurry and from a tidal viewpoint the later we were the better, but going slow in a swell is a good way to set off seasickness: Ian didn't look too comfortable and I'd just found out that my anti-seasickness device, last used in the Bristol Channel, had a flat battery. With the more positive motion induced by a couple of extra knots we felt a little better, and we started to enjoy the sights around the Forth. The Isle of May disappeared astern, a tanker passed us on its way out of the Forth, a ferry or cruise ship crossed in the opposite direction and a container ship headed north. Off to the south-west Bass Rock loomed out of the haze, a massive stone rising from the water. Then with two knots of tide against us we closed slowly on St Abb's Head, an impressive lump of rock with a lighthouse complex atop it. I called up Eyemouth harbour to check conditions, we dropped the mainsail, and we prepared to enter just after one o'clock.

The entrance to Eyemouth involves keeping two markers on the harbour pierheads in line to approach safely between some offshore rocks. In a swell or rough sea it takes a fair amount of nerve because the harbour entrance isn't visible until the very last, when a turn opens up into a narrow gorgelike passage running between John Smeaton's original breakwater and another built parallel to it in the 1960s. I piloted *Indalo* in with plenty of care, entered the upper harbour as instructed in the pilot book, and berthed next to *Dart Dash* who had arrived earlier direct from Arbroath. Ian's wife Flora drew up shortly after and he prepared to be whisked away back to Dundee and on to the Highlands. I said farewell on the pontoon then went off to explore the town.

Eyemouth dates from the twelfth century and it was once an active trading port and an important fishing harbour. It still boasts a fleet of around eighty vessels and a fairly active fish market, though there was little going on there today. It's also a minor holiday resort with a small and noisy beach to the north of the harbour, but away from that the town is pleasant and compact with a fair range of everyday facilities, shops and hostelries. I could get washing done, get fuel and supplies and even order some batteries for my anti-seasickness watch that would be delivered in the morning. It wasn't exactly Kyleakin or Helmsdale, but it wasn't a bad place either.

I was determined to get into Berwick so once I was back on board I made a more thorough examination of the echosounder. The problem was that the sounder unit hadn't exactly come loose, but it wasn't very well bonded to the hull. It sits in the bottom of a locker that it shares with some toolboxes and other bits and pieces, and my guess was that it had been disturbed by an errant toolbox in a rough sea and it was now having problems 'seeing' through the hull. I pulled the unit out and cleaned it up, then re-stuck it with silicone sealant. To protect it from flying toolboxes I made up a protective wall out of some timber I had on board, fixing it in the corner of the locker with a white paste that was supposed to Stick Like S**t. I crossed my fingers and switched the gauge on: it read 1.8 metres. Pleased with my efforts, I had a chat with Keith on *Dart Dash* and treated myself to a seafood dish and most of a bottle of wine in an Italian-themed bistro on the opposite side of the harbour.

Monday 25th July, day 73, was technically my last day in Scotland. It seemed an age ago that I'd made landfall in Port Ellen, but somehow the time had gone quickly too. When I arrived in Berwick I would be two-thirds of the way around and back in England (undisputedly, as Berwick's dock is on the south side of the Tweed). Nevertheless it still seemed as if the most difficult parts were yet to come, for though I'd negotiated Cornwall's Atlantic coast, rounded Cape Wrath and traversed the Pentland Firth, parts of the east coast are nearly as unforgiving and many of the harbours become inaccessible if the wind drives ashore. Even for the prudent there's plenty of scope to be delayed as well as being bumped around on exposed quays like the one at Stonehaven. More positively I'd be joined by my next crew, Abi, in a few days' time, then I'd meet Janine in Grimsby and Pat on the south coast for the run home.

147

The tides weren't right for Berwick until mid-afternoon so I spent the morning refuelling, trying without success to get my washing washed, and enjoying the best shower I'd had since Oban. I'm not normally a fan of cooked breakfasts and usually prefer a cereal bar and a cup of tea, but for once I called into the Fishermen's Mission and ordered some sausages, bacon and toast. They had a Mission newspaper that included a short article on Eyemouth and in particular the storm of 1881, so I sat reading about one of the worst recorded fishing disasters off the British coast when an October gale sank twenty-three boats and claimed the lives of 189 local fishermen. Then I skimmed through a section on uniforms for merchant seamen and wondered if being skipper of *Indalo* entitled me to wear anything more exciting than a standard dinner jacket and cummerbund. Next I moved on to the story of a Russian ship that had been sunk in New Zealand, according to the Russians by the negligence of the local pilot. I finished my breakfast before getting to the end of the story so I never found out why it happened or whose fault it was.

By the turn of the tide the sun was out and there was a gentle breeze, but the swell coming in from the northeast had if anything strengthened. There's only about nine miles of open sea between Eyemouth and Berwick so I told myself it shouldn't be too bad. I negotiated the gorge and the rocks to get out of the harbour then quickly turned into the open sea with the tide in my favour and the swell on the port quarter. Burnmouth appeared in the cliffs then the Farne Islands came into view to the south. Before long I had Berwick abeam, lining the lighthouse on the breakwater up with what I hoped was the spire on the town hall and not one of the churches. I turned in to the mouth of the Tweed while keeping an eye on the echosounder. Straight along the breakwater, then hard to port at the beacon: keep a pair of marks in line and watch the depth, then bear away to starboard and follow the navigational buoys in to Tweed Dock on the south bank. As I reached the dock I realised that what I'd assumed were hundreds of seagulls on the river were actually swans. I'd never imagined to see so many together in one place.

Tweed Dock was basically a commercial basin with a few cranes and a lorry park on the quay, half a dozen small fishing boats tied up in one corner, and a single yacht in the one yacht berth. There was no sign of any commercial activity. The yacht was a UFO called *Mercurian*, about the same size as *Indalo*. I hailed the crew and tied up alongside, immediately being invited to join them in the evening for a pint or two in a pub called the Barrels Alehouse. First things first I decided to walk around the walls of Berwick and find somewhere for dinner.

I'd never before visited the 'walled burgh,' but I'd heard plenty about it and imagined it might be something like Chester or Londonderry or maybe one of the French walled towns like the old part of Granville in Normandy. From the dock there's a short walk through Tweedmouth along a matter-of-fact street with a few shops and cafés, then over the river via the seventeenth-century Old Bridge to Berwick. Crossing to the town I found it was quite different to what I'd expected as the old walls had been replaced in Elizabethan times, so if anything it brought to mind the Garrison on St Mary's in the Isles of Scilly. Tall stone mediaeval walls look nice and they are good for firing arrows and throwing rocks from, but they can be reduced to rubble by cannon fire and Elizabeth (and her predecessors Mary and Henry VIII who actually ordered the new walls to be built) wanted something that could withstand artillery. So in the greatest engineering project of Elizabeth's reign Berwick's walls were rebuilt lower and thicker as earth ramparts with stone faces and bastions, and garrisons and military stores were set up inside the town.

From the perimeter the town itself looked a compact and characterful place but I resisted delving into the centre until I'd been all the way around, a distance of about a mile and a half. Finally I backtracked to the western gate, walked a little way outwards along a road called Castlegate, then returned beneath the arch where it became Marygate and led to the town hall and the churchlike clock tower that I'd identified from the sea. Berwick's centre is busy and bustling, the eastern side serene, the riverside intimate. Castlegate made me think of Oxford and the back alleys on the river side of the town reflected something remotely French, slightly reminiscent of St-Malo, or perhaps it was just my imagination. Bridge Street, Hide Hill and Sandgate were, well, just Berwick: ordinary streets, no cobbles or sets or anything fancy, but not quite like anywhere else. I took it in for what it was and realised this unique place had lived up to my expectations, and more.

Starting to feel hungry I wandered down towards one of the riverside gates and examined some menus, eventually choosing a restaurant called Popinjays that had an Oriental chef and did a good Malaysian chicken curry. Berwick's Englishness was showing through here, as outside the bigger towns and a few select pubs Scotland had seemed a bit limited in choice of cuisine. Having eaten I dropped into the Barrels and was soon joined by Archie, Dave and Billy from *Mercurian*. The Barrels was a good real ale pub, something else that had been in short supply in the east of Scotland. Having finished our first round we moved temporarily to the Brown Bear, an establishment I'd spotted earlier and marked down as interesting. It didn't do real ale but it was old, traditional and it had escaped obvious renovation. Then we returned to the Barrels, and finally to *Mercurian* for a nightcap.

Next day I let *Mercurian* out to head home to Eyemouth, then I went off to continue my exploration of Berwick. The town has the dubious accolade of being the most fought-over settlement in Europe, changing hands between the Scots and the English a total of fourteen times. Originally Scottish, it was granted a charter as a royal burgh by David I in 1141 which started its rise to prosperity. By the thirteenth century

Berwick was a major trading port for the North Sea with merchants from the continent setting up warehouses and building villas there. The peace and prosperity was short-lived however, and Edward I of England sacked the town in the first Anglo-Scottish war, installing a garrison and building the first set of walls to keep the Scots out. Robert the Bruce captured it in 1318 and strengthened the walls against the English, only for it to be retaken a mere fifteen years later. After several further changes of side it went to Scotland in 1461 after the Wars of the Roses, until it was captured yet again for England in 1482 by the future Richard III. Fifty years on the walls were reported as in need of repair, and Henry VIII ordered their strengthening and Mary their remodelling into their present form. Not that that was the end of the story, for during the Civil War Berwick was variously occupied by Royalists, Parliamentarians and Scottish Covenanters.

After the Union between Scotland and England matters should have been straightforward, but they weren't. Legally Berwick was described as 'of' England but not 'in' it, leading to oddities that included a century-long state of war with Russia. The declaration that started the Crimean War in 1853 was signed by "Victoria, Queen of Great Britain, Ireland, Berwick-upon-Tweed and the British Dominions beyond the sea." But when hostilities were brought to a close three years later at the Treaty of Paris, Berwick was left out. Cold War notwithstanding Berwick and Russia made peace in 1966.

Today Berwick retains something of a split personality. Administratively of course it's English, though its county of Berwickshire is part of the Scottish Borders region. Its football team plays in the Scottish league, and looking at the souvenir shops visitors could be excused for thinking it's firmly in Scotland. The River Tweed, which is regarded as Scottish and for most of its length forms the border between the two countries, runs south of Berwick and divides the town from Tweedmouth. All of this might not matter too much now we have the United Kingdom and the European Union, but some south of the line envy the Scots their more generous healthcare and education arrangements, and there are those to the north who think the town would sit better in the Scottish Borders rather than in English Northumberland. There may even have been a referendum if the English north-east had voted to set up a regional assembly in Newcastle, but it didn't and there wasn't. Either way I didn't put my Scottish courtesy flag away until my second day in port, though I was wrong anyway as I was berthed on the southern side of the river and undisputedly on home ground.

Incidentally Berwick was a favourite haunt of the painter L S Lowry, and there's a Lowry trail in the town illustrated with his paintings and sketches at the relevant points so that they can be compared with the scenes today. Lowry often visited between the 1930s and his death in 1976, staying in the Castle Hotel. To my mind his style suited the industrial scenes he is famous for rather than the Berwick townscape, though some of his drawings do capture the spirit of the place rather well.

After collecting some provisions I had afternoon tea in a tea-shop and walked back by way of the 'new' 1920s Royal Tweed Bridge to get a better view of the railway viaduct, one of Robert Stevenson's last works. Back at the harbour the swans were all crowded into the dock and clustered up in one corner like a flock of sheep. I took a few pictures then turned my attention to the navigation for the next day, down to Blyth where I could experience the hospitality of the yacht club and get my washing done. I plotted the tricky bit inside the Farne Islands and picked out some possible ports of refuge along the way, for good measure adding a pilotage plan for the Tyne a little further on. Then Abi called about meeting up, I had a chat with a truck driver who was parked on the quayside for the night, and, ready to begin the final third of my voyage, I turned in.

9

Castles, Monkeys and Cod

I awoke in Tweed Dock at three in the morning looking forward to my first passage of more than forty miles since leaving Scrabster. I slipped the mooring at four, stowed ropes and fenders and put the mainsail up in the shelter of the dock before motoring out into a serenely calm River Tweed. As I headed out to sea a slight swell came in from the north-east, producing a gentle rocking motion rather than anything unpleasant. The flattish Northumbrian coast was lit up in pastel early-morning hues with just a shimmering of mist, and to the east the sun broke free of a wall of sea-fog and illuminated a steely-blue sky. I set a course just outside of Emmanuel Head on the northern end of Lindisfarne, and as I approached it the island gradually took on a form distinct from the mainland. I passed a white obelisk daymark on the headland, now glinting in the sun, and altering course in a double dogleg *Indalo* came safely between the Farne Islands and some miscellaneous rocks on the landward side.

Opposite the Farnes looms mighty Bamburgh Castle, one of the most magnificent fortifications on the English seaboard and the site of what was once the capital of Viking Northumbria. The present castle dates from shortly after the Norman invasion, though much of it apart from the keep was destroyed by artillery fire and what's seen today is largely the result of eighteenth- and nineteenth-century restorations. The castle served more as a deterrent to the Scots and a base to check the activities of border outlaws than as a defence from seaward, and the best-known story about Bamburgh isn't a siege or anything but its role in the escape of Thomas Forster. Lord of the castle at the beginning of the eighteenth century, Forster threw in his lot with the Earl of Mar's promising Jacobite rising of 1715. He led part of the earl's army in a successful attack on Preston, but following some tactical mistakes he lost the advantage and surrendered. He was thrown into Newgate Prison from where he was rescued by his sister Dorothy through a ruse where she disguised him as her maid. And I thought it only happened in films. Anyway, Tom laid low in Bamburgh for two years before sailing for France from nearby Waren Burn (or Waren Bum if you believe the castle guide).

From Bamburgh I had a straightforward run down the coast passing in sequence the craggy ruins of Dunstanburgh Castle, Boulmer where an RAF 'yellow budgie' was doing its exercises, the little Coquet Island off Amble, and Newbiggin-by-the-Sea and its conspicuous power station. Next came some wind turbines announcing that I was approaching Blyth, one of the north-east's most active sailing centres. A yacht race was in progress off the town, the first time I'd seen sails in any number since the Sound of Mull. But the day was sunny, I was enjoying sitting out keeping watch and I didn't feel like going in to port quite yet. Remembering my conversation with Iain from *Rainbow Catcher* when we were holed up in Badachro, I wondered if I could find a berth in the Tyne. I knew Newcastle was hosting the Tall Ships Week but there could just be a chance of getting into one of the marinas further downriver or berthing on the fish quay at North Shields. I checked and Royal Quays had some space though I'd have to pay dearly for it. I used to have relations in North Shields but I'd never taken the opportunity to visit, so at least I could find out what the place was like.

Just past Blyth I was hailed by a small fishing boat and directed to alter course around a small buoy. Between the Farnes and the Tyne I counted perhaps a dozen of these, basically open wooden boats with a tarpaulin of some sort stretched over a simple frame to make a tent over the forward part of the vessel. They were traditional Northumbrian salmon boats fishing in more or less the same way that they had done for centuries, the procedure being to string a long net between two buoys to catch the salmon migrating along the coast. In between setting and hauling the net the fishermen keep watch and warn off any boats that are in danger of tangling themselves up.

I entered the Tyne about at about half-two, though it took another hour and a half to get through the busy lock into Royal Quays and tie up. I took my washing to the facilities block, had a beer in the beer tent that they had set up for Tall Ships Week, rang Abi to let her know where I was, and when the clothes were done and dried I went off for a walk into North Shields. At first the route was circuitous and not very attractive, the direct path along the river blocked by a derelict and fenced-off piece of land. The town itself was OK in a down-to-earth sort of way, a bit scruffy here and there but not too rough or depressed. The fish quay was interesting enough and it had good views over the mouth of the river, but the pubs seemed to be for drinking in rather than eating and the only restaurant I could find, a cosy-looking Italian, was fully booked. So I resigned myself to a pizza in the marina beer tent and set off back towards the town centre. Before I'd gone far I stumbled across a pub called the Magnesia Bank that I'd bypassed on the way up. It was still doing food and there was live music due to start any minute, so I placed my order and sat down to be entertained for an hour by a light rock outfit called The Twilight Zone. All in all a good find, but I never did find out if the pub's name commemorates part of the Tyne, a financial institution or a stock of stomach pills.

On Thursday I was due to meet Abi at a metro station a mile or so north of the marina. The day started wet and miserable, but it wasn't bad enough to deter a crowd of people from lining the quay to watch the Tall Ships procession. I joined them for a moment: first came the 1930s Norwegian 676-tonner *Christian Radich*, then a small trad-itionally-rigged ketch that I couldn't see the name of, next Britain's sail training vessel *Tenacious*, launched in 2000 and the biggest wooden sailing ship in commission, and finally before I had to pull myself away the rather elegant *Pogoria* from Poland. Leaving the marina I walked around the dock and through a landscaped area with paths and water running through it (a 'green wedge' I think the planners call them), then I got lost in a nondescript suburb. This part of North Shields is designed for car drivers and for cyclists using cycle paths and green wedges, but nobody seems to have thought that pedestrians might want to cut through the housing estates to find metro stations. Eventually I found a station called Percy somebody-or-other which wasn't the one we'd agreed on, but after a few text messages and phone calls Abi got off at the right stop and we met in a big and rather empty pub where I'd gone to get out of the rain.

In the afternoon we took the metro into Newcastle. Once the great powerhouse of the North, the city declined in the second half of the twentieth century to reach a seriously low ebb. More recently it has undergone something of a re-naissance that even if it hasn't revived the town's industrial might has at least given it the feel of a buzzing regional capital and pushed it to the top of the list for city breaks. We found our way into the centre from the main station and wandered around in the rain, suitably impressed by the blocks of rather grand and elegant Georgian buildings. Down by the river the huge Sage concert hall came into view, a big glass and steel building shaped like a short fat caterpillar or the end of one of those contoured condoms. A little way further on was the Millennium Bridge connecting Newcastle and Gateshead, better known as the Blinking Eye. It's made up of two light arched spans, the top one canted just off vertical and the bottom one a walkway describing a flattish curve as if it were the shadow of the other. When the bridge lifts the lower arch is raised on cables towards the upper one like, well, a blinking eye.

As the rain got heavier we looked for a refuge and found a smart modern bar called 55 Degrees after its latitude. By the end of our first drink the rain had eased a little, so we set off again to explore and found the New Castle that gives the city its name. This squat and solid-looking keep is all that remains of the city's twelfth-century castle. Originally built to subdue the rebellious Northerners and hold off the Scots, the stone castle replaced a wooden structure put up after the Norman invasion. In its turn it was superseded by the city walls, which have since been largely demolished leaving the keep as one of the few reminders of a fortified Newcastle. The structure looked in exceptional condition for its age until we learned that most of the stonework had been replaced within the last hundred years.

Too late to get into the keep we headed off to the Bridge Hotel, a traditional Newcastle pub that we'd had a recommendation for. I should mention at this point that Abi is secretary of one of the Camra branches and likes a decent pint or two or three, at least when she isn't trying to slim. The Bridge was a characterful spot and the beer was good, but there was no food on offer so we had to make alternative arrangements before catching the metro back to a damp and misty North Shields. Even in the rain we found a lot to like

about Newcastle, not least its friendly no-nonsense feel and
the easy way it combines the old and historic with the new
and trendy. With the weather looking as it did I wondered if
we would be back the next day. We could at least bring *Indalo*
with us and tie up on one of the city-centre pontoons now the
tall ships were gone.

Friday morning was still wet and the forecast was for a fresh
or strong northeasterly, perhaps a near-gale, with the sea
building to rough. Plus we had the proverbial fog on the
Tyne. Undeterred we decided to leave North Shields after
lunch and go to Hartlepool if the weather improved,
Sunderland if it didn't, and Newcastle if we got outside and
didn't like what we saw. As we emerged into the river
visibility was dismal and whole place felt eerie, with ship's
horns sounding in the distance. We spent fifteen minutes sat
in the shallows waiting for an outbound ship to pass with its
retinue of a pilot boat and two tugs, followed by a further ten
just inside the entrance while another one came in. I judged
that we could see just about far enough to be safe so long as
we stayed inshore away from big ships, so we headed out
around the breakwater and turned south. There wasn't any
wind at all but the swell was impressive, and before long Abi
was feeling queasy and I was content to go into Sunderland.

I'd already plotted GPS routes into Sunderland and
Hartlepool that would keep us safely to the starboard side of
the respective harbour mouths and out of the way of any
traffic coming out. I activated the Sunderland option to take
us up to the outer breakwater, across to the inner one, and
onwards to the marina. A noise like a beast with an elephant-
sized stomach-ache announced that we were approaching the
first breakwater, the structure itself looming out of the fog in
front of us. I steered *Indalo* close to its tip then followed a
bearing across the outer harbour, the second breakwater

appearing exactly where the GPS said it would be. From there the marina entrance was visible so we motored in carefully, called the office on the radio and tied up in a vacant berth. I immediately took a liking to the place: it was on a smaller scale than Royal Quays and surrounded by a not unattractive housing development that gave it a more intimate feel. The facilities were better too, and without the Tall Ships event to hike the prices up it was a good deal cheaper.

With *Indalo* safely secured we set off into Sunderland. We took the most obvious route along a main road and over the Wear bridge, an impressive single arch in green-painted iron dating from the 1920s. The city centre was a mix of modern and functional, old and modestly grand, smart and peeling. It seemed friendly and high-spirited without so far as we could see the threat of drunken violence that mars too many town centres on a Friday and Saturday night. Maybe that would come later in the evening, or perhaps people around here are just better at enjoying themselves. We consulted the Good Beer Guide from *Indalo*'s library (a gift from Abi on a previous trip) and found a selection of recommended pubs. Asking around suggested that Fitzgerald's was the place to go, so we found our way there and sampled the local brew in suitably traditional surroundings before retracing our steps to find a place to eat. Having got a favourable impression of Sunderland we set off back across the bridge, now lit up in shimmering green in the drizzle, and discovered a sculpture-lined riverside walk past the university and back to the marina.

Saturday's forecast was no better than Friday's so we decided to stay put and see more of Sunderland. Our first stop was the National Glass Centre, close to the river and a short distance upstream from the marina. Long before Sunderland became associated with cars or even shipbuilding it was Britain's pre-eminent centre of glass production. Back in the seventh century the abbot of nearby Wearmouth monastery invited some French craftsmen over to make glass, though it took another thousand years for the city to become a centre of serious manufacture. If you have a Pyrex dish, unless it's an imported one it will have been made in Sunderland at the Jobling glassworks where Pyrex has been made since 1920. The museum started off with a bit about the town's history, then there was an exhibit of how glass bottles were recycled, though I wondered why we couldn't just pay a deposit on them and give them back to be washed and re-used like we did when I was a child. Next was a gallery of hands-on exhibits that turned us into a couple of overgrown kids for half an hour. When we'd tired of pushing buttons and manipulating levers we toured the glassblowing and forming facilities and Abi, still in big kid mode, blew a glass bubble.

The glass centre also houses a gallery of art made in glass, some of it for sale. My favourite exhibit was a set of imaginary creatures arranged in a circle. They looked rather like jellyfish or maybe sea anemones without the tentacles, and going around the circle they changed from a cylindrical blob through a series of funnels to a stud-shaped organism and back to a cylinder again, the creature turning itself inside-out in the process. I didn't have anywhere to put them where they wouldn't get damaged so I didn't buy the exhibit, and I also forgot to write down the artist's name.

After the glass centre we walked into Sunderland for the second time in the rain. We split up to have a better look at the town centre, meeting back in Fitzgerald's. My first impressions were reinforced: this isn't a bad place at all. The port was once, and this now seems incredible, the British Empire's busiest shipbuilding centre, but along with the trade in coal that kept the quays busy all the activity has now gone. Two tall dockside cranes stand proudly on the quay but there's little left for them to do. I'm not sure what's replaced all the heavy industry, though Sunderland doesn't look as run-down as I expected. Nissan to an extent maybe, and a few corporate headquarters are starting to appear too. Back on board I checked in my English guidebook and this important northern city doesn't get a mention. The index goes straight from sunburn to surfing, neither of which were likely to feature today.

The next day the weather was slightly better, and having explored as much as we wanted in Sunderland we decided to brave the swell and go. A look outside the harbour told us the sea was uncomfortable but manageable, so we took on some fuel and set off mid-morning with the tide. It was still rather misty and the heavy swell hadn't gone, so we settled for Hartlepool rather than the longer haul down to Whitby. For the first time since Arbroath there was a good sailing wind, a moderate to fresh breeze from astern, and we made good progress under mainsail alone. I steered in the swell while Abi took a seasickness pill and tried unsuccessfully to catch mackerel with a trolling line.

The Durham coastline that we were sailing past used to be one of the most derelict and polluted in Britain; anyone who can remember the 1970s film *Get Carter* (the original, not the remake) will have an idea of what I mean. Blighted by coal sludge and industrial waste and used as a garbage dump it had become seemingly beyond salvation. Then in the 1990s a programme was begun to restore it, and today the twenty-mile stretch from Sunderland to Hartlepool bears little trace of its industrial past, or not that we could notice from our perspective of alternatively rising up on the wavecrests and dipping into the troughs. It wasn't as interesting as the Northumberland coastline, but it wasn't bad.

In Hartlepool we had the choice of the original harbour that's close to the old town centre but lacks facilities, or the locked modern marina in West Hartlepool. We chose the soft option, dropped the sail, trickled in towards the lock, and promptly dropped a fender overboard. Watched by a small crowd on the quayside I turned *Indalo* about and deftly hoiked it out of the water with a boathook while Abi put out the rest of the fenders and the ropes. No applause for my efforts, but we were soon through the lock and tied up in one of the harbour's several basins. The marina is huge and there's still a lot of space not occupied by pontoons or boats. One of the quaysides has been developed as the 'marina village' with bars, restaurants, a couple of shops, and the toilet facilities and office. Given the sunny afternoon it wouldn't have seemed out of place in a Mediterranean resort. I'm not particularly keen on big marinas but this one is well-designed, well-run and welcoming.

Once tied up we decided to take a walk that would eventually bring us out on the opposite side of the lock, visiting on the way the town centre, the station, and the maritime museum and its two historic ships. The centre seemed very quiet on a Sunday afternoon for a town of a hundred thousand people, but it was rather neat and this part of Hartlepool was quite smart and pleasant, not the run-down ex-port that I'd half expected. We found the station, again very low-key, Abi worked out her departure plan, then we walked around the back of the harbour to have a look at HMS *Trincomalee*, the oldest British warship still afloat. She had been built from teak in India in the early nineteenth century and taken out of service in 1857, eventually being restored in Hartlepool in the 1990s; as a result the town now has an almost unrivalled set of skills in ship restoration. Close by is a rather newer vessel, the paddle steamer *Waverley Castle*, one of three built in Hartlepool in the thirties for the Humber ferry service. The others are the *Lincoln Castle* that's now on show in Grimsby and the *Tattershall Castle* that serves as a floating pub at London's Charing Cross Embankment.

Having arrived too late to go on board either of the ships we had a look around the little maritime museum, which was very well presented and divided itself between sea life and the maritime history of Hartlepool. The old town dates back at least to 647 AD, and its abbey was built only a few years later. West Hartlepool grew up much later with the construction of the new harbour and the coming of the railway. It became a major fishing port, then a centre of engineering, steel manufacture, shipbuilding and sea transport. Shipbuilding and rig construction had gone by the end of the 1970s, the amount of coal going through the docks fell off at the same time, and the last steelworks and engineering plants closed in the eighties. Hartlepool won a City Challenge bid in 1992 which helped to construct the marina and surrounding developments, though I'm not sure how much income and employment it will bring. Already there seem to be empty buildings and while the town and the harbour are commendable it isn't in the best location to become a major yachting centre.

A rather grotesque story connected with Hartlepool explains the figures of monkeys that appear all over the place in various guises. It goes something like this. During the Napoleonic wars a French ship was wrecked off the town and the only survivor was a monkey that came ashore with the wreckage. Some local fishermen captured the unfortunate creature and decided to try it for being a French spy. Quite naturally it couldn't speak English to defend itself, so they found it guilty and it was hanged. Sadistic or simply dim the fishermen might seem, but there may have been a motive to the hanging. The story isn't exclusive to Hartlepool and other versions suggest the fishermen decided to eliminate the last survivor so that they could claim the wreck as salvage. Whatever the truth, the monkey has become a sort of town mascot; there's even a brass one by the lock gates. Maybe Hartlepudlians should be called monkeys in the same way that Jerseymen are crapeaux and Guernseymen ânes.

On Monday Abi was due to meet a friend in Thirsk, so after she left to catch the train I was back to single-handed sailing. I cleared the lock at half-past ten and pointed *Indalo* to the south-east for Whitby, twenty-five miles down the coast. There was little wind and the swell was less than it had been, but I had the tide in my favour and it didn't seem long before my destination was in sight. Whitby is protected by two detached breakwaters that act as baffles at the protruding harbour mouth – I could describe the shape anatomically but I won't, but take a look on a large-scale chart or better go there and walk up the 199 Steps to see it from above and you will see what I mean. Nevertheless the harbour opens to the north and a heavy swell can make for dangerous conditions in the entrance. Several other boats were converging on the harbour as I approached and the leaders had no problem getting in other than rolling a little, so I followed them. A large crowd lined the quayside, but before I could take a bow or wave some flares around I realised I was being followed by the *Grand Turk*, star of the *Hornblower* television series and a frequent sight in Whitby.

Abi and her friend Anne were among the crowd so I did get a welcome directed at me, and after negotiating a swing bridge and playing musical chairs with some other boats to get a berth I joined them in the town and arranged to meet up a bit later for a drink. After Berwick, Whitby was the place I'd most wanted to see on the English east coast. The town has been a renowned fishing port for a thousand years, it's had a lifeboat for the last two hundred, and it's the place where Captain James Cook started his maritime career in 1747 as an apprentice seaman on the coal ships or cats. Whitby also attracts superlatives for its fish and chips, its back streets, and its ruined abbey where the seventh-century Synod of Whitby was held to end the split between the Celtic church and the Church of Rome. The crow's nest was invented in the town two hundred years ago by William Scoresby, one of Britain's most successful whaling captains, and Bram Stoker stayed there for a while and used it as the scene for part of *Dracula*. And there's a gallery full of evocative pictures by Frank Meadow Sutcliffe, a photographer who captured Whitby just before its maritime heyday came to a close at the end of the nineteenth century (it was a Sutcliffe photograph of a stranded Russian ship that inspired the opening part of *Dracula*, where the count comes ashore from a shipwreck in the form of a dog). Finally, Whitby used to have a jet industry: not the aeronautical kind, but the black stone that was dug out of the cliffs and made into ornaments. In the nineteenth century it supported two hundred workshops, in the twenty-first there are none.

Despite all this history my strongest impression was of a crowded holiday resort. As it was a warm and sunny August day the town was swarming with holidaymakers and there was hardly room to move on the quays. Even bigger were the hordes of seagulls, outnumbering even the swans at Berwick. I made my rendezvous with Abi and Anne then I had a look around some of the back alleys, crossed the harbour by the swing bridge and ascended the 199 Steps to the abbey. After taking in the views I descended again and explored the back alleys on the east side. The Cook museum had already closed (although he didn't move there until he was eighteen the town has adopted him as its most famous 'son'), so I decided to head away from the coast and escape the crowds. I took a walk along the river, over a modern main-road bridge with views back down the harbour, and then back along the other side. I didn't feel like fish and chips so I bought some food at the supermarket and cooked on board ready for departure in the morning. I felt I was being unfair on Whitby to leave so quickly, but now the weather had improved I wanted to be out at sea and on my way.

The tides and the swing bridge dictated that I should leave at 0450 on the dot, giving me a straightforward passage out of the harbour and into the North Sea. A puff of wind close offshore fooled me into thinking I was going to sail, but it soon evaporated into a barely perceptible whisper. The gentle sweep of Robin Hood's Bay curved away to starboard, then the bold shape of Scarborough Rock appeared further down the fossil-rich coast. I'd decided to make Bridlington my next port of call, making an anchor stop halfway to wait for the tide. For my stop I chose Filey, where a pointed headland called Filey Brigg and the rocky causeway extending beyond would make a good natural breakwater against the remains of the swell. I turned in a respectable distance past the causeway, gave a wide berth to two small fishing boats that were laying nets, and dropped my anchor in just under three metres of water.

After a couple of hours snoozing in the cockpit I awoke to a hot and sunny day. Filey beach was crowded, fishing boats pottered to and fro, and a small fleet of sailing dinghies were being readied for launch from another beach just below a little wooded ravine in the side of Filey Brigg. It was too pleasant to move on straight away so I made a cup of tea and relaxed watching the dinghies while I drank it. Eventually my navigator's conscience got the better of me and I upped anchor and set a course for the distant shape of Flamborough Head. As I approached the headland the cliffs at first appeared dark, then a light brown, and finally almost white as I rounded the Flamborough lighthouse and they caught the sun. I tucked in between the coast and the buoy that marks the northern end of Smithic Shoal, a long offshore sandbank running south roughly parallel with the shore, and headed towards Bridlington. I couldn't raise anyone on the VHF so I got ropes and fenders ready, entered the crowded harbour, and tied up to a yacht from Grimsby that had arrived a few moments before. The harbourmaster appeared on the quay, warned us that the harbour dried out to soft mud, took some money and left us to it.

Having secured my lines both to my neighbour and to the quay I tidied up and went ashore. Bridlington was once a regular port of call for coasters and colliers, but apart from a small fishing fleet and several day trippers it's now mainly a centre for yachts and leisure boats. Most of the resident yachts berth in the middle of the harbour in wooden cradles that keep them upright when the tide goes out, something I've not seen anywhere else in Britain though apparently it's not unique to Bridlington. The town is a popular holiday resort and has all the normal seaside paraphernalia, but in some ways it's delightfully old-fashioned and reminiscent of what seaside resorts used to be like when I was a child. There's even a place called the Rock and Novelty Shop, which I didn't go in but supposed sold rock and novelties. And that, with the addition of a shower, a pie and a glass of wine, was my experience of Bridlington.

I slipped my lines a fraction before six in the morning and left the harbour to face an adverse tide. Not that the current mattered very much because my destination, Grimsby, is entered through a lock. Arrive too early and you can't get in, arrive a little later and there's a fee of £10, or arrive at freeflow and it's free. Anyway, there was slight southwesterly blowing so I put the sails up, and as I coasted down the side of Smithic Shoal it had me pressing the button to silence the engine. Before too long it increased to a moderate to fresh breeze. I could have hammered along under full sail, but wanting to decrease *Indalo's* speed I put two reefs in the mainsail and rolled the foresail down to the size of a storm jib. Despite being set up for a wind a couple of notches higher I was still doing nearly five knots through the water, almost six over the ground once tide had turned. Ironically now that there was a decent wind I couldn't make proper use of it.

The coastline south of Bridlington is much less dramatic than the stretch down to Flamborough Head, levelling out first to low cliffs and bluffs and then to sand dunes, heralding the low-lying Lincolnshire coast to come. The clay bluffs are gradually being eaten away by the sea and behind them lies the flat and vulnerable plain of Holderness, forty miles long and fifteen deep. Not a particularly interesting coast from seaward though it may appear differently ashore. On board I was surprised to notice that I'd acquired a passenger, a rather tired-looking pigeon that had stolen aboard when I wasn't looking and was now nestling on the coachroof between the liferaft and the rubber dinghy. It took a wary interest in my goings about on board, but otherwise it just sat there with its feathers fluffed up, its gaze following me around the cockpit. Concerned that I'd behead it when I gybed the mainsail I stretched out to move it somewhere safe, but the bird thought better of being manhandled and flew off in the direction of the shore.

Fifteen miles out of Bridlington *Indalo* crossed over the Greenwich meridian and temporarily entered the eastern hemisphere. I set a course to take me about three miles east of Spurn Head, the long peninsula of sand-dunes that marks the southern limit of the Yorkshire coast, so that I could approach the shipping lanes in relatively safe water and then turn west to run parallel with them into the mouth of the Humber. I identified the buoys marking the edge of the shipping route and turned into the wind, realising that it was now at the strong end of fresh. It would be dangerous to tack to and fro across the shipping channel so I furled the foresail and motored in. If I thought I'd be more sheltered in the estuary I was mistaken: the wind picked up and there was a sudden squall of heavy rain. I made a dogleg to cross the shipping lane, then turned into a second squall that the port radio channel told me was blowing at force seven. I was struggling to hold much more than three knots, the spray was flying and the rain was hitting my face like warm hail, but it wasn't cold and I was nearly into port so I wasn't complaining.

Grimsby is marked out by its distinctive Italianate-Victorian hydraulic lock tower, a square pencil-like structure that looks as if it could have come out of the set of *Lord of the Rings*. After what seemed an interminably long half-hour battling wind and spray I closed with the harbour mouth, crossed back over the zero meridian, and headed in. It was a quarter past four, already freeflow, so I called the harbour and went through into the yacht basin. I spotted a vacant pontoon belonging to Humber Cruising Club and a kindly yachtsman came out of the clubhouse to help me tie up and tell me where the facilities were. Once I'd settled in I rang

Janine, my next crew, only to find that she would have to be excused the next passage as she had a badly sprained shoulder. Her next chance to join me would be at Lowestoft or Yarmouth in a few days' time.

Grimsby is supposedly named after a tenth-century Danish fisherman called Grim, though Grim is also another name for the Norse god Woden or Odin (as in Grime's Graves or Grim's Holes in the Norfolk Breckland) so it could have been called after him instead. Either way I decided to spend the next day in town to see if it really did live up to its name. My first impression was that it might, as the marina is in one of the Fish Docks and though there's some commercial activity going on the whole area looks run-down and scruffy. From the docks I took a road to what I thought was the town centre, a slightly down-at-heel shopping street. Eventually I was pointed to the real centre which was smarter and cleaner if somewhat anonymous, and I found my way to a pleasing café in a small and peaceful precinct. I had a leisurely lunch of haddock in parsley sauce, then I went to look for the town's National Fishing Heritage Centre.

Grimsby was once one of England's greatest fishing ports with at its height over 550 boats, many of them deep-water trawlers. When the railway arrived in the middle of the nineteenth century it gave the town an impetus to develop as a fish-landing and processing station, a function it has made its own: it now handles a million tons of fish a year, more than five times the whole of the British quota. I'd assumed that it was still a major fishing port, but it isn't any more and rather ironically much of the catch brought for processing arrives and leaves by road. Grimsby was part of the same story as Wick, Peterhead, Aberdeen and Hartlepool, but along with Hull it also suffered disproportionately from the 'cod war' of the 1970s, when Iceland increased its territorial

169

limit first to fifty and then two hundred miles. I have images from my childhood of British trawlers being chased off by Icelandic gunboats only to return under the protection of British frigates. The posturing was ended in 1976 when Britain recognised the Icelanders' new limit in return for limited fishing rights. At the time there were still five hundred trawlers operating in the Humber and a third of the population of Grimsby worked in fishing or in the industries that depended on it. Almost nine thousand Humberside workers lost their jobs as a result of the Icelandic action, and the long decline of Grimsby as a fishing port had begun.

As a young lad who knew no better I naturally supported the British against the Icelanders' presumptuousness in extending their territory, and I felt a certain amount of pride about the Navy stretching out its long arm and protecting the livelihoods of our fishermen. Now I realise what the Icelandic government was up to I applaud its foresight. According to ICES, the International Council for the Exploration of the Sea, there should be at least 150,000 tonnes of cod in the North Sea to maintain a healthy stock. In fact there are less than a third of that and plaice are becoming scarce too, though at the moment there are plenty of haddock. Both ICES and the Royal Commission on Environmental Pollution have called for a complete ban on taking North Sea cod. The European Union recently made a small nod in the right direction but it fell far short of what's needed. In fact part of the blame for letting the situation get so bad in the first place must go to the EU's Common Fisheries Policy. This agreement has operated as something as a free-for-all and discouraged anyone in particular from taking responsibility for the fish stocks: if we stop fishing in the North Sea the Spanish or the French or someone else will come in, and vice-versa in their waters. Iceland is one of the few places in Europe that's got sustainable cod stocks. Surely it's time for us to follow suit and manage our fisheries properly, even if the short-term costs are hard to bear. The alternative should North Sea cod continue to decline is that we will lose half our white-fish fleet with no foreseeable hope of recovery.

Back to the Heritage Centre. The main part of the Centre consists of a series of tableaux reconstructing life in different parts of a 1950s trawler, such as the trawl deck, galley, nav station, cabins and so on, as well as aspects of the shore-based life of the fishermen. It's all highly atmospheric, particularly the part with the fishermen hauling nets and sorting the catch on a freezing Arctic night. Anyone with any romantic notions about the life of an offshore fisherman will soon lose them here. Excellent though the centre is, there wasn't much about the cod war or the decline of the cod stocks or anything at all so far as I could see about overfishing.

Outside in the dock were the *Lincoln Castle*, the paddle-steamer made in Hartlepool, and the *Ross Tiger*, a retired trawler. Neither were open and the time was getting on so I called in at the supermarket next to the centre before wandering back to the boat. Grimsby, I decided, wasn't all that grim, but it wasn't very memorable either.

171

10

East of Greenwich

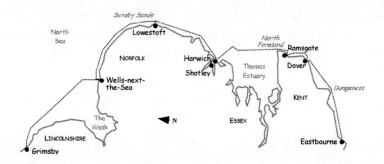

Sailing south-east from Grimsby there are two choices. One is to make the hundred-mile passage across to the Norfolk coast somewhere off Cromer and around to the all-tide ports of Great Yarmouth or Lowestoft. *Dart Dash* took this route a few days back, but for a single-handed sailor it means about eighteen to twenty hours on watch, more if anything goes wrong. The alternative for a relatively shallow-draft boat like *Indalo* is to stop off at Wells, a fifty-mile leg that needs careful timing to have enough depth to get over the sand-bar in the entrance. I had picked up some information on the harbour before setting out in the spring and I'd also discussed it with the local yachtsman I met in Whitehills. So I chose to split the passage at Wells, though I kept my navigation notes for Lowestoft and Yarmouth handy just in case.

The lock in Grimsby dictated leaving within two hours of local high water, and to get over the shallows into Wells I wanted to arrive between an hour and a half and half an hour before high water there. Allowing for the biggest range of possibilities I left at half-past seven and emerged back over the zero meridian into a flat-calm Humber, very different to the scene that had greeted me two days before. This time I followed the recommended yacht track to the south of the main shipping channel, but there were no vessels on the move other than a couple of fishing boats leaving just ahead of me. A short way out of port I passed a tanker moored to the Tetney Monobuoy: this floating structure, like a big red navigational buoy with some appendages stuck on here and there, carries the oil pipeline to Tetney terminal and allows ships to moor up and offload without coming inshore and berthing on a jetty.

Three hours after leaving Grimsby I was fully clear of the Humber estuary and its shipping channels and I could set a course for a waypoint that I'd marked on the chart a few miles north of Wells. The flat Lincolnshire coast had faded to a thin, uncertain line, while over to the south what looked like a series of islands gradually became visible. Slowly they joined up to become the indented and sandbank-bound west Norfolk coastline. In contrast to the eroding eastern seaboard this section of the shore is silting up through a process known as longshore drift. Sand is picked up by the sea further east and deposited in spits and sandbanks along the coast, gradually cutting the harbours off from open water. Several villages that are now a mile or more inland, places like Stiffkey, Wiveton and Salthouse, once had harbours of their own. The same process is happening at Blakeney, Wells and Brancaster. Wells recently lost its coaster trade because the harbour entrance became too tortuous and shallow, and while fishing boats and yachts can still get in they need to time their arrival carefully. I didn't anticipate any problems in *Indalo*, but a deep-keel yacht like *Dart Dash* would need to pass over the shallows within perhaps half an hour of high water if she were to get in at all.

As I reached my waypoint a baby seal surfaced and turned on its back, looking at me like an amused child. Surprised to see it I smiled back. Turning due south I worked out that I'd arrive an hour and a half before high water, ideal as I'd be entering on a rising tide. I made out the first pair of red and green buoys at the mouth of the Wells channel, then spotted the red and white fairway buoy that marks the correct line of approach. I dropped the mainsail, got ropes and fenders ready, and called the harbour on the VHF to see if there was anyone around to guide me in. There wasn't, but a homeward-bound fisherman hailed me and said I could follow him. The shore had a subtropical appearance: pine trees on sand dunes and a dune island with clean sandy beaches and nobody on it. Even the beach huts weren't the standard type and suggested something mildly exotic. The channel wound through the sand then seemed to disappear entirely, a line of buoys eventually revealing that it continued around the back of a sand spit. Inside the harbour the winding route carried on up to the quay, where I tied up and waited for *Indalo* to squelch out on the soft mud.

I'd never visited Norfolk before and knew nothing about Wells other than what I'd gleaned from the pilot book and my friend in Whitehills. The foreshore of pantiled houses made for a picturesque setting, though closer up it was slightly marred by the usual seaside stuff. I would like to have strolled along the dunes that I'd passed coming in but they were a fair way from the quay, and my priority was having something to eat before getting an early night. So I headed in the opposite direction, into the village centre where I discovered the Edinburgh Hotel. I had an excellent fish pie with a pint of heavy ale called Railway Sleeper; given that there was a funfair over the road from the quay I hoped it would live up to its name. Wells was a pretty enough place, but it was full of holidaymakers and seemed to be succumbing a little to seaside tat. Like Whitby, it might be better out of season.

I awoke on Saturday morning to find *Indalo* stuck nose-down in the mud. The forecast was good with a moderate to fresh westerly or northwesterly, which would give me some onshore swell but a good sailing wind too. So I prepared for the sixty-mile leg to Lowestoft, the easternmost town in Britain, and hoped that the boat would float free in time to catch the tide. Half an hour later she was sitting level on the rising water and I could set off. Slipping out of my berth at half-six I made my way back along the twisting channel into what had become a moderately rough sea. I hauled the main-sail up, bore away on a run with the wind in the west, un-furled the foresail and settled down to steer manually in the swell.

Indalo isn't the best boat for sailing downwind as the foresail flaps around in the lee of the mainsail, while the way the rigging is arranged stops the mainsail from being let out at a full right angle to the boat. I tried rolling the foresail away and continuing under main alone. After a couple of hours of hand steering I wanted some automatic assistance, and after fiddling unsuccessfully with the windvane I just about managed to get the autopilot to steer with the engine on. The wind was fickle, starting with a gentle breeze, freshening for a while, then dropping back to a force three, then a six or strong breeze for a couple of miles, and finally back to gentle or light. I went back to manual steering with the mainsail, tried unfurling the foresail for a few miles, returned to the engine and autopilot, shortened the mainsail, let it out again, gave the foresail another try, then finally I gave up and motorsailed.

The Norfolk coast is more interesting than the flat, monotonous line of Lincolnshire: low sandy cliffs here, sand dunes there, taller cliffs around Sheringham and Cromer. Sheringham nestles in a gap in the cliffs and looks tempting from seawards though unable to offer refuge to an eight-metre boat. It's about here that the longshore drift stops and erosion begins: not far away a steamer called *Victoria of Yar-*

mouth once went aground on submerged Shipden church. Then the coast becomes flatter, punctuated by radio masts and a power station, before giving way to the rather hum-drum seaside that runs down to Great Yarmouth. To the seaward side lies the Scroby wind farm, a large evenly-spaced cluster of turbines on the just-submerged Scroby Sands. They make a strange sight, the first group of turbines I'd seen on the voyage. Individually they are things of interest and maybe elegance, but I'm undecided if groups of them in the water are a welcome sight or not, at least on this coast; I'm sure I'd object in the strongest terms if anyone tried to put them in Mount's Bay or Loch Alsh.

When I left Wells I had a fair tide all the way around the northern coast, but as I approached Scroby it turned against me with a vengeance. I was at the Cockle navigation buoy, sixteen miles from Lowestoft, at one in the afternoon. Five hours later I still wasn't in the harbour, the tide reducing my progress to little more than walking pace. Eventually I called Lowestoft Harbour Control, got clearance to enter, and at half-past six I rafted up to another boat in the Royal Norfolk and Suffolk Yacht Club's marina. Deciding to wait until Sunday to go into town I confined my shoreside activities to the showers, bar and restaurant in the attractive century-old clubhouse. It had been a long day: twelve hours at sea to do what the GPS reckoned at 59 nautical miles over the ground, though the log added another eight to that fighting the tide.

In the morning I set out to explore Lowestoft. The town is in two distinct parts, with the main centre situated on the north side of the river and the seaside resort on the same side as the marina. I called in at the tourist office for a map, which they eventually produced, but they seemed much better equipped to help me if I wanted to go to Norwich in Norfolk rather than staying in Lowestoft in Suffolk. I crossed over a bridge to the far side of the harbour and found what looked like the coast road, but it was separated from the shore by a strip of industrial units and car showrooms. After a mile or so going north I gave up on seeing the coast and walked inland and south again, eventually coming to an architecturally drab shopping precinct. So I meandered back over the bridge and walked down a road that ran parallel with the beach, cutting through a side street to the sea front before it left the town.

Eventually I found my way to a pub called the Harbour Inn for a late lunch, sitting below a sign that said the last good herring catch was over forty years ago. Once there were seven hundred herring drifters and a good sprinkling of smokeries in Lowestoft but now there are none. And talking of fishing, the harbour is home to a trawler called the *Mincarlo* that's open to visitors. I'd planned to look around it to make up for missing the *Ross Tiger* in Grimsby, as well as finding out why an East Coast trawler is named after a rock in the Scilly Isles. But I arrived too late to go on board, and I never discovered the answer.

I set out off for Harwich at 0625 on a rather chilly Monday morning, just ahead of my neighbour who was doing the shorter passage to Aldeburgh and could afford to wait for the tide to turn in his favour. I called port control for clearance, motored out of the harbour entrance, and logged the eastern-most point of the voyage at 1°47′.0 E before turning to starboard. Once I'd cleared the offlying sandbanks I hoisted the sails and headed south along the coast with a gentle to moderate northwesterly behind me. Southwold soon came into view followed by Sizewell power station just to the south of it, dominating the coast for the next couple of hours. Though I couldn't see it my chart told me I was passing Dunwich, a stark reminder of the erosion that's taken place on this coast. In Saxon times Dunwich was a thriving town of five thousand people, but in 1326 the sea destroyed four hundred houses and three churches and blocked the harbour entrance. By the end of the seventeenth century it had reached the town centre, and in 1919 the last of the town's twelve churches fell. Dunwich might still be on the map, but it's holding on by its fingernails.

Passing Sizewell I let a ship alter course to give way to me, then I rounded Thorpe Ness and brought Aldeburgh into view, a pretty town with coloured houses facing the sea. Another victim of erosion, it has lost two or three streets to the waves since mediaeval times and the distinctive Moot Hall that once marked the town centre is now almost on the beach. Nevertheless Aldeburgh has the advantage of backing on to a flat sweep of sand rather than sitting perched on a cliff, and the rate of erosion is much slower than at Dunwich. I'd been there briefly as a child and I would like to have called in, but entering means going another ten or twelve miles along the coast to negotiate a tricky entrance into the River Alde and then backtracking inside the long sand spit of Orford Ness. I thought better of it.

Orford Ness made itself known by its radio masts and lighthouse, alerting me to change course slightly and trim the sails to head in towards Harwich. I was looking for a green navigational buoy called Cutler, which would be the signal to turn further to starboard to head for a distinctive green pillar that marks the edge of the shipping channel into Harwich. Then I'd turn to port and cross the shipping lane, passing a few boat-lengths behind a big Norfolk Lines freighter. Turning on to the recommended yacht track into the dual Orwell / Stour estuary meant coming head to wind, so I took the opportunity to drop sail and motor. Nosing around Harwich I found a yacht pontoon in the town centre at a place called Halfpenny Quay, but it looked uncomfortable with the wind blowing straight on to it so I called up Shotley Marina on the opposite side of the river and locked in there for the night.

Shotley is a large, long, well-equipped marina tucked in behind an artificial bank at Shotley Point, the place where the Stour and the Orwell go their separate ways. It's not far from Shotley Gate village but it's self-contained with an extensive facilities block, small shop, restaurant and so on, and none of the usual marina development flats or houses. It's also, and my eyes lit up when I found this out, one of the few marinas that have baths. That could wait for later though: first I caught a ferry to Harwich to have a look around and buy some provisions. I'd expected a large, busy, not very salubrious town and found instead a rather village-like, olde-worlde centre with a few shops, an impressive church, several B&Bs and pubs, and the Electric Palace, a little cinema built in 1911. Harwich is on a peninsula like a smaller-scale version of Falmouth so I walked a little way inland, crossed over to the south side, then walked along the sea front and back around to the quay where I stopped off for a coffee before catching the ferry again. Harwich Harbour is the busiest container port in Europe, but most of the cargo is handled across the river in Felixstowe leaving Harwich itself in relative peace.

After doing some small jobs on the boat I took a walk along the Stour into the village of Shotley Gate and came back on a footpath across some fields. Behind the marina is the abandoned and decaying remains of HMS *Ganges*, a training centre for naval cadets that was used for about seventy years up until the 1970s. I noticed that a planning application had been made to build houses, shops and business units on the site, and there were a few posters saying 'Ganges – Not Finished Yet.' Something needs to be done with the Ganges site, but I'm not sure that adding a big new estate on to a small and probably peaceful village is really the answer. Back at the marina I had a meal in the bar, spoke with a man who was on the side of the posters rather than the developers, left a message for Janine to see if she could meet me in Ipswich, then for only the second time in the voyage treated myself to the luxury of a long, hot bath.

Tuesday started bright and sunny, with just enough cloud and breeze to make it nicely warm rather than unpleasantly hot. Before I left the boat for the morning Janine rang back to say there was no improvement and she would be staying away from sailing for a while. So I would be single-handed as far as Brighton, though we arranged to catch up socially on the south coast. I'd already decided to go into Ipswich, but now that Janine wouldn't be coming I opted to go by road rather than taking *Indalo* upriver. The bus from Shotley Gate wound through pleasant if flat rural and village scenery before depositing me in the centre of town, and I sat next to a woman who was originally from Somerset but had moved to Shotley because her husband had got a job locally. She didn't seem too keen on the Ganges proposals either.

In town I bought a few things I couldn't get in Harwich and strolled around to get a quick impression of the city, Suffolk's county town. Ipswich is a busy place with plenty of shops and eating-places and it has enough old buildings to make the streets vaguely interesting. Not by a long way a Chester or a York, but worth a lunchtime visit. And talking about lunch I spotted a sign saying 'Church's Bistro' and wondered if it was a converted church along the lines of the one in Aberdeen. It wasn't, but it was next to a church and it was well-presented and had an interesting menu. I ordered three starters and a cold beer, and sat outside opposite the leafy church grounds enjoying a slow repast while I started on a book I'd just bought about French society and culture.

Back at Shotley I left the marina and headed a short distance up the Orwell to Levington. I wanted to see if I could find a boat called *Hespere* that belonged to Mary, someone who had sailed with me in Cornwall a couple of years ago. I found her (*Hespere*, not Mary) tied to a buoy, so I came along-side and went aboard to have a look. I thought about picking up one of the spare buoys in the river for the night, but it would put me a fair way from the sea for tomorrow's early morning start and I really wanted to stretch my legs. So I motored back down to Harwich and berthed on Halfpenny Quay, going ashore for a quick pint before putting the final touches to my plan for crossing the Thames on Wednesday.

As a Londoner by birth the Thames is in a sense my home river, though I have never sailed in it and I've only ever been on it perhaps three or four times on trip boats and ferries. I'd considered going upriver and berthing in Limehouse Basin or St Katharine's Dock just to say I'd been into the capital, but it would be a big detour to visit a city that I saw often enough on business. Now it was within reach the idea didn't appeal very much.

The Thames would also be something of a watershed, the last big estuary I had to cross, the last open stretch of water before entering the English Channel, and the passage that would give me a toehold on the south coast. Arriving in Ramsgate would put me on the home straight with less than two hundred and fifty miles left to go. But I wasn't there yet, and the Thames is one of the trickiest estuaries around British shores with strong tides, sandbanks and busy shipping lanes, and like the Tyne it has more than its fair share of fog. When I was planning my voyage the forty-five mile crossing of the Thames was one of the sections I wanted to make sure I had crew for. Now with Janine unfit and no chance of a replacement I was on my own, but from close up the river seemed much less daunting than it had on paper.

On the chart the estuary looks challenging mainly because of the sandbanks and shallows that radiate out of the river mouth. If conditions had been rough I would have gone right out and taken the big-ship route around all the shoals, adding perhaps ten miles to the passage. But the forecast was favourable, and I drew three straight lines that would take me safely from the mouth of the Orwell all the way to Broadstairs on the east Kent coast. The first line ran from just outside Harwich where the recommended yacht track takes a ninety-degree turn to seaward. It would take *Indalo* south of Cork Sands and across various shallows and channels to the end of Sunk Sand, a long semi-submerged ridge. Then I would take a dogleg five miles to the southwest along Black Deep, one of the main shipping channels. The final line started on the northern side of Black Deep, crossed over to a buoy marking the end of a narrow north-south channel known as Foulger's Gat, ran the three miles through the Gat, then crossed the open water of the southern Thames over to the North Foreland and beyond to Broadstairs, where I could start turning in to join the approach channel to Ramsgate. That was the theory, and it looked easy.

The nights were longer by four hours now than they had been a month ago in the north of Scotland, so while an 0300 start would have put me in a good approximation of daylight back then, now I needed to wait until five in the morning to be sure of seeing any hazards in the water. I beat my alarm by five minutes and left at 0455, with enough light to see by save for the dazzling effect of the dock lights on the Felixstowe side of the river. The weather was fair and the sea only slightly disturbed so I followed my plan and took the short cut across the shallows. The sun rose about an hour after I came out of the river-mouth, silhouetting the strange shape of a ship's cargo stacked on the sea, the hull all but invisible below the horizon. I held my course to the head of Sunk Sand, turned on to the dogleg just as an incoming freighter came past, then an hour later picked up the buoy at the head of Foulger's Gat and turned south again. As I sighted its counterpart at the far end of the Gat the Essex coast had already faded into the haze astern and Kent began to appear ahead as a broken line of cliffs.

The southern half of the Thames estuary was a busy and sunny scene of ships at anchor, fishing boats going about their business and the odd yacht or motor cruiser motoring around. The cliffs and then the towns of the Kentish coast stood out in the sun forming a varied panorama that contrasted with the flat coastlines of Essex and Suffolk. I had a strange and unexpected feeling that I was making a proper landfall as if I had crossed a sea rather than an estuary, perhaps arriving back from France or the Scilly Isles. In a sense I was crossing back home into the southern strip of England, making the reciprocal passage to the one I'd done ten weeks before across the Bristol Channel from Padstow. Passing the bright cliffs of the North Foreland and turning into Ramsgate I somehow felt I was back on familiar ground, back onto my own stretch of coast, even though I'd never been to the town in my life nor sailed further east along the Channel than the Isle of Wight.

It was hot and still in Ramsgate so I treated myself to a cold beer and a shower before taking a look ashore. From seaward Ramsgate's sea walls, cliffs and terraces looked intriguing, giving a hint that this could be a walled town. It's not but it is perched on the top of the cliffs, and getting into the town itself meant climbing several steep flights of steps followed by a short walk to the centre. The climb was worth it just for the view over the inner harbour and the older, lower part of the town that surrounds it. I've heard Ramsgate described as an English Monte Carlo without the glitz, and there's definitely something reminiscent of the Mediterranean about the place; it's not, as I'd half expected, just a run-of-the-mill holiday resort. Ramsgate is neither pretentious nor scruffy and it has a fair range of eating-places and watering-holes as well as what looks like a fairly well-equipped shopping centre. There wasn't enough to make me want to stay another day, but it was a good place to make my Kentish landfall.

On the clifftop I stopped to read an information board. The harbour started its life in mediaeval times or earlier as a rough haven made by fishermen to shelter their boats. In the middle of the eighteenth century Parliament decreed that the harbour should be strengthened as a port of refuge to try to reduce the number of ships going aground in storms on the notorious Goodwin Sands. The resulting works were successful, but even now the Ramsgate lifeboat is one of the busiest in the country. George IV visited in 1821 and gave it the unique title of Royal Harbour, though it doesn't warrant a King's or Queen's Harbourmaster like Plymouth or Portsmouth. By the nineteenth century Ramsgate was a busy merchant port and to a lesser extent fishing haven, but today it's mainly occupied by yachts and ferries with a few fishermen to keep things going.

If it had stayed a little warmer into the evening there was an attractive terrace of cafés overlooking the sea with outside seating. I was still considering sitting inside one of them when I remembered that there was an Indian restaurant that had been recommended a few years back in one of the yachting magazines. As I hadn't been in an Indian since Wick I decided to search it out. Luckily the first one I found still had the article in the window so I didn't have the embarrassing problem of asking whether it was the right one. I was the only person in there and the food, while perfectly acceptable, didn't prompt me to take up my pen and write a review for *Yachting Monthly*.

I sat on a bench overlooking the harbour to let my dinner go down, watch the sun set and contemplate the voyage. In coming south I realised that I'd returned to the world of big marinas and anonymous boats, underpinned maybe by a way of life that's itself more anonymous than it is in the Scottish highlands or even somewhere like Berwick or Aberystwyth. It's harder to find neighbours to share experiences with and rather than being one of a small band of voyagers I'm just another person parking a floating caravan in a big caravan park. In Shieldaig, Scrabster and Helmsdale we were *the* visiting yacht, in Kinlochbervie, Berwick and Aberdeen one of two. In Thurso I was made to feel like a minor celebrity to be sailing off the wild north coast, and in Lossiemouth I was asked if *Indalo* could have a mention in the local paper. In Aberdeen it was a source of conversation to say I'd arrived by boat, as it was in Berwick. Down here I may as well have turned up in my Renault Mégane. I know marinas aren't the only places to moor on the south coast, but for heading homewards along the Channel they are the most convenient as the drying harbours like Sandwich and Rye don't really work with a west-going tide. At least I liked Ramsgate. I wasn't sure I was going to feel the same about the big marinas in Eastbourne and Brighton.

From Ramsgate my choices were to start at 0430 and make a sixty-mile passage to Eastbourne, half of it against the tide; set out mid-morning for Dover; or stay put for another day. I could also go over to France, though at the risk of being locked up and having my boat impounded as I hadn't brought my passport. Dover won. In my original planning I hadn't intended to stop there as it's not even twenty miles from Ramsgate, but it did make for an easy passage and somehow it seemed wrong to miss it. This is the closest port to France, the 'key to England' according to mediaeval historian Matthew Paris, and the place where all the tides are calculated from: know the time of high water Dover and you can work out what the tide is doing anywhere in Britain to within half an hour or so. It's also the busiest ferry port in the world, and more to the point for a visit it has a castle that at least rivals Bamburgh's.

It was already hot when I left at ten in the morning, so for only the fourth day of my trip I was in T-shirt and shorts. There was barely a breeze, but again the Kentish coast offered scenic cliffs, wide beaches and behind them interesting settlement-scapes. Deal came into view, then a little later I was passing the South Foreland with the White Cliffs of Dover gloriously reflecting the sun. It was too hazy to see the French coast but its direction was revealed by the constant stream of ferries plying in and out of Dover harbour. I wondered how I would get in. *Pas de problème*: I called Port Control, followed their instructions and slipped in as soon as the next Sea France ferry had left. As I crossed the mile-wide outer harbour a working boat was using a crane to dredge up mud from the sea bed. It brought to mind one of those penny cranes in amusement arcades that you manipulate to try to pick up a sweet or a toy car or another penny or something, except that this one was actually managing to pick stuff up.

Once I'd checked in at the marina I went off for a walk around Dover. The town's main beach is inside the harbour, with the inner harbour running a couple of hundred yards behind it roughly parallel with the sea front. I walked up the beach hoping to find a café overlooking the front, but there were only apartments, houses and hotels, as well as a yacht club which did have a terrace though not a very enticing one. Ramsgate was an exception to the rule but on the whole Britain isn't very good at making use of waterfront. If there's a terrace café to be found it's often got car parking between it and the water, or if it does occupy a prime position it turns out to be the kind of greasy spoon place that should have car parking in front of it. Behind the front was a retail complex that had a sort of terrace but the café was unexciting and anyway it looked over a car park, not water or anything interesting. Some of the signs in Dover are bilingual, but I was beginning to despair of any other continental influence having rubbed off here. Finally in the town centre I found two cafés overlooking the central square (or 'round,' as it was like a pedestrian roundabout) with canopies and outside seats in the French style. Almost satisfied, I sat outside one and had a French beer and an Italian ciabatta.

At the far end of the beach overlooking the commercial ferry port is Dover's mighty castle. Even from a distance it looks massive, though it appears as more a collection of ramparts and buildings than a single imposing structure like Bamburgh. I wandered up Castle Street and met a Canadian woman who was also on her way to the castle, walking with her up to the ticket kiosk. The admission fee was rather steep and they didn't accept my National Trust card, but the views over the port and town were worth half of it. I parted with my Canadian friend, who wanted to see the tunnels that had been used to plan the evacuation from Dunkirk during the second world war, and headed up to the keep and the best views.

After a browse around the keep I was persuaded to take a rather intriguing tour through an audiovisual display. It described the defence of the castle in the thirteenth century, part of an important event in England's history that I knew virtually nothing about. It starts with King John's reluctant signing of the Magna Carta at Runnymede in 1215. This charter was a kind of constitution that limited the king's powers without the agreement of his barons, but no sooner had the ink dried than he started to ignore it. From the barons' point of view there was only one thing to do: depose John and replace him with a king more inclined to listen to them. Their choice was Prince Louis of France, later Louis VIII, who landed an army at Sandwich in May 1216. Louis was welcomed into Canterbury and within a month he had control of the key towns of London and Winchester. By July only Dover and Windsor stood in his way. At Dover Louis cut off supplies to the castle, brought in siege engines and undermined one of the towers. The castle was almost lost but the resourcefulness of the garrison and its able commander Hubert de Burgh held the invaders at bay and forced a temporary truce. Nevertheless the tide was in Louis' favour and but for John leaving the scene when he did England's history may have taken a very different course. The king fell ill after a banquet, and by the middle of October he was dead leaving his nine-year-old son Henry on the throne.

Now that the object of their enmity was gone the barons had less reason to back Louis, so his support started to wane. Needing a quick victory the French prince stepped up his campaign and made another attempt to take Dover a year after his first landing. Once more the castle held firm, though this time the siege was short-lived. Louis' northern army suffered defeat at Lincoln, and a few days later his plan to

187

bring in more troops from France was thwarted. As the French ships made their way across the Channel they were intercepted off Sandwich by a much smaller fleet mustered by de Burgh. The English manoeuvred to windward of the French, normally not a very clever tactic in thirteenth-century ships. But Hubert knew what he was doing: when the enemy were within range, he let fly with quicklime, blinding the French sailors and giving his archers the advantage. Left with a strong force but with little hope left of seizing the English crown, Louis accepted a large ransom and went home.

When I'd seen all I wanted to see in the castle I walked back into town and followed the inner harbour down to the bridge next to the marina. Most of the waterside was car park (more poor land use), but at least there was a harbourside footpath a little further down with some planters alongside it. I walked along it to find that the gate at the end was bolted shut and the bolt had rusted in place. Why have a footpath, plant flowers next to it, and then lock it off so it doesn't lead anywhere? Then I noticed a gate into the harbour that was opened by a keypad lock, so I tried the code I'd been given for the marina. It worked and got me on to a pontoon, from where I could get back out on to the road near the bridge. On the opposite side I discovered Cullin's bar and bistro backing on to the harbour with a few patio tables overlooking the water, undisturbed by traffic or parked cars. I sat and had a drink while I wrote out a postcard, admired a big old-style yacht that was moored opposite, and studied a booklet I'd picked up in the castle.

⚓

So that was Dover. The next morning I checked the 0500 forecast before starting an hour later for Eastbourne in a moderate northwesterly, giving me a fairly comfortable sailing angle as far as Dungeness. I'd pictured this headland, the triangle on the map that projects from the southern coast of Kent, as a flat piece of land with perhaps the lighthouse becoming visible before the coast itself. What I actually saw was a large power station that appears long before the land or even the lighthouse. On a passage westwards past Dungeness it's difficult to carry the current for more than four hours, so I'd timed my departure to have the tide with me for the central section where it's strongest. I swept past the headland with an extra knot and a half from the current and turned as close as *Indalo* would go into the breeze. The wind wouldn't quite let me make a direct line for Eastbourne, and with seventeen miles to go my speed had dropped to less than four knots and I was two and a half miles south of where I wanted to be. I furled away the foresail, brought the engine into play, and set a course for Sovereign Harbour that just about allowed the mainsail to fill.

Eastbourne's harbour is a large complex two or three miles north-east from the centre of town. The outer part is tidal and it's protected by breakwaters and watched over by a Martello tower. From this entrance bowl there's a lock giving access to the inner harbour and marina, off which there are three more yacht basins that can be reached when swing bridges are opened. The whole thing looks as if it might once have been a set of commercial docks like West Hartlepool, but it was actually built at the beginning of the 1990s as a leisure port, a hundred years after the local council first proposed creating a harbour for Eastbourne. The entire complex is surrounded by the usual marina development houses and flats, though some of the houses off the north dock are quite spacious and attractive (and no doubt expensive), each with its own piece of quayside. There's an area of bars and restaurants called the Waterfront, with a few shops around the back and an out-of-town shopping centre and cinema a short walk away. The place has the artificial feel of being planned in one go, but having said that it's self-contained, reasonably well thought out, and there's enough there to keep the unadventurous visitor happy for a week.

Once I'd got organised I rang Janine to say I was in Eastbourne and she arranged to come over that evening for a meal. I tidied up, had a shower in the excellent facilities block, and wandered over to the Waterfront where I sat on the terrace with a welcome glass of cold beer. We ate on the patio of a Thai restaurant simply called the Thai Marina, sitting in enormous sculpted wooden seats. The food was excellent. Janine was sorry to have missed the sailing, but we agreed to meet for an outing later in the season when she was in better condition. Another phone call revealed that my next crew member also had to cry off as her father was about to go into hospital, so unless I heard from one of my other sailing friends I was single-handed now for the rest of the voyage.

I spent the weekend in Sovereign Harbour, Saturday intentionally to catch up on domestics and provisioning and generally have a lazy time, and Sunday because of a poor weather forecast. I shopped in the local supermarket, an Asda. I have nothing particular against Asda or their produce, but for some reason the ones I've been to get full of people who dawdle around, block the aisles with trolleys (or with themselves), stand in front of whatever it is I want to buy while shouting at their kids, and generally behave as if they're entitled to hog the whole shop. Eastbourne Asda was no different but it did have most of what I wanted. And though I checked carefully there were no overweight people hanging around the back smoking, no shopping trolleys in the harbour and an impressive shortage of litter.

Back at the boat the weather worsened. To keep out of the rain I stayed on board writing an article for a yachting magazine, heated up a quiche for dinner, and looked at the navigation for the next passages. My next move would be the fairly straightforward run around Beachy Head and into Brighton. After that I'd make a landfall somewhere on the Isle of Wight. I liked the idea of Bembridge, a drying harbour on the island's north-eastern corner, but arriving there with enough tide to get in would mean setting out from Brighton around midnight, stemming the tide until Selsey Bill, then making a dash across to the island. I considered Cowes instead: a couple of hours further on but accessible at all states of the tide. Cowes is crowded at the height of the summer and has a habit of filling up for yachting events, so I'd need to check in advance that there would be space.

Sunday was windy but not too wet, ideal for a look around Eastbourne. It was also the last day of the Airbourne, Eastbourne's summer air festival, so I might be able to spot some aircraft going over. The three-mile trek into town along the sea front was advertised as a fitness walk with information boards at regular intervals claiming that they were to motivate less fit people to continue walking. It wasn't a very interesting walk and they might have added something to stop fitter ones throwing themselves in the sea. I suppose there was a small flotilla of boats out to sea to look at while they were bouncing around in the waves looking at the air display, and a few small fishing boats drawn up on the beach. A couple of other unusual features also tried to liven the walk up: first there was a lowish building made up of tiers and part-circles that I hoped housed a theatre or restaurant or museum or something but turned out to be the local water treatment works, and then closer to the town there was a redoubt, a lowish circular fort with various old cannons and second world war guns looking out from it. Inside it there was another floor below ground level that contained a museum. I made a mental note to revisit on the way back.

The sea front and esplanade were packed with people watching the air display, so I wandered inland. Eastbourne town centre was bigger than I expected it to be and it goes back quite a long way from the sea front. There were some individually interesting old buildings and a small, fairly attractive area of local shops, but overall the impression was quite mundane: nothing exactly wrong with it but nothing very exciting either. After a pub lunch I tried to find a more interesting part of town. According to the signposts there's an

Old Town somewhere but it seemed to be up in the Sussex Downs and I gave up and walked back, this time along the inland road that would take me back to the harbour shopping area. The road was busy and boring, about par for the course, and in my lack of enthusiasm for Eastbourne I forgot to revisit the redoubt. A look in an estate agent's window revealed that this was the first place I'd visited since Dartmouth where property prices were more than at home. I don't know why; if I had to make the choice I'd rather live in Sunderland.

Eventually I spotted the Asda, walked around the back of it (still no litter) and crossed into the harbour area. Looking at my Airbourne programme there should have been a Spitfire flying over at 1520, but nothing had happened by half-past so either it was called off or the plane kept very low and stayed around the pier. I gave it another ten minutes, then strolled back to the boat to finish the navigation. My final act in Eastbourne was to give the dinghy, or rather its motor, some exercise. I'd last used it six weeks ago in Badachro and outboards that don't get used regularly have a habit of becoming difficult to start. It's something to do with the petrol in the two-stroke mix evaporating and the oil that's left behind gumming up the spark plug and the carburettor. Anyway, as if to chide me for my lack of faith the little Tohatsu started first pull, and to round off the day I zipped under the footbridges for half an hour of exploring the North and South Harbours.

11

Homeward Bound

The forecast for Monday was sunny with a light breeze, so I could make my escape from Eastbourne. The day started bright if hazy, and I was up and through the lock by 0735 to meet a slight sea and a gentle breeze. I hoisted the sails but the wind was only good for three and a half knots, so as I passed the town pier I started the engine and got on my way. Eastbourne itself sparkled white in the morning sun as if to tempt me back, but I followed the line of the cliffs down to the infamous Beachy Head. At 160m the headland is the tallest chalk promontory on the British coast, though lit up by the sunlight it lacked any of the brooding malevolence that can haunt the granite outcrops of the south-west. Nevertheless I kept a good offing as according to the chart it doesn't plunge cleanly into the sea. Turning the corner brought me head to wind, so I rolled in the foresail and carried on under main and engine. I still had fifteen miles to go to Brighton but it was an easy run and I sat back and admired the view: first the Seven Sisters, then a break where a stream disgorged

193

from the South Downs, then Seaford and the entrance to Newhaven. The GPS tripped through the zero meridian in line with Peacehaven as *Indalo* passed back into the western hemisphere, then Rottingdean came abeam at the end of the cliffs followed shortly after by the breakwaters of Brighton Marina. I dropped the mainsail, ticked into the marina after a little less than four hours at sea, and tied up.

Brighton's marina is a completely artificial creation made by extending two breakwaters out into the sea beneath the cliffs. The result is a veritable yacht city: the biggest artificial leisure harbour in Europe with a huge expanse of water and pontoons, enough to accommodate 1500 boats. It's well-organised with good facilities, cheaper than Eastbourne, and it manages to have the relaxed feel of an upmarket holiday resort. There are the normal marina development apartments but this time they have been designed to add something to the setting. The terrace above the marina is also well-designed; it's nothing special but it has a variety of bars, cafés and restaurants, there's plenty of outdoor seating, and there's no traffic to spoil the view. Behind the terrace is a large and architecturally varied precinct of shops, pubs, restaurants, leisure and entertainment facilities, as well as an enormous supermarket (another Asda) at the very back where it's least obtrusive. As a large, self-contained marina complex this one works rather well; I'm not saying it can't be improved, but others could learn from it.

The downside is that the marina isn't really made for pedestrians to get out of. The service roads are about as complex as those leading to a medium-sized airport, and they have to be crossed or got under to walk out. There's an ugly and oversized concrete zigzag path to go up the cliff, but overall the impression is that people are expected to use wheels rather than feet or else stay put and patronise the waterside establishments. I got as far as the top of the cliff but decided I didn't like the look of the road going into Brighton and headed for the shingle beach instead. A little train was pulling into a similarly scaled-down Victorian sea-front station, so I strolled over to it and bought a ticket. The narrow-gauge single-track railway line was built by Magnus Volk in 1883 and it was the first electric railway in the world. It has two trains running along it that pass at a central station, and it makes for a slow but pleasing way to travel along the sea front to Brighton pier.

I'd only been to Brighton once before, on business, and I wasn't quite sure what to make of it. The town started to grow out of a fishing village called Brighthelmstone when Richard Russell, a doctor from Lewes, wrote a book on the virtues of sea-water and encouraged people to bathe off the beach. It became a smart and fashionable resort particularly after the future George IV visited in 1783. At some point however it went downhill quite badly and in my childhood it was among other things the scene of Saturday night battles between Mods and Rockers. Since then it's pulled itself up to be a thriving centre of arts and culture as well as becoming one of the first clutch of places to be conferred with the status of a civil city. Nevertheless I'm still in two minds about it.

I walked into the Lanes, little back-streets housing cafés, artists' studios and antique shops, then had a look at the Pavilion and its gardens. This Oriental-style extravaganza was designed by John Nash for the flamboyant Prince Regent and built between 1787 and 1822. The exterior influence is Mughal and the interior Chinese, though I was too late to go in and see it. The Lanes, the Pavilion and the Dome give Brighton a feel that recalls some of the better bits of London. The London-by-the-Sea analogy continues into busy, dirty roads and some less salubrious parts of town, as well as more positively a huge choice of places to eat and drink and a few venues for the more cultured forms of entertainment too. Brighton is undeniably more interesting than Eastbourne, but though I'd liked to have looked inside the Pavilion it couldn't tempt me to stop for an extra day. So I caught a bus back to the marina and sat outside one of the waterside restaurants.

I left Brighton for the Isle of Wight at six in the morning, having been assured that there would be plenty of space in Cowes. To begin with the coast was obscured by haze, but as the morning wore on the visibility improved along with the temperature. As the haze cleared I made out Littlehampton and then a little further to the west Bognor Regis. Bognor was one of those quieter holiday resorts that appealed to my parents (as well as to George V who gave it its epithet), and I have memories of childhood holidays where we based ourselves there and explored the Sussex countryside and coast. A building stood out on Bognor's sea front like a miniature version of the Millennium Dome, though neither my chart nor the Bognor entry in my English travel guide revealed what it was. A little further on I looked in vain for Pagham Harbour, a natural haven that's too shallow for anything but a dinghy or a punt and is now a nature reserve. The entrance was somewhere among the low-lying shingle dunes, but it was invisible even through the binoculars.

By mid-morning the sun was out in full force and I stripped down to shirtsleeves, shorts and bare feet once more. A pleasant smell of countryside, like flowers and hay, wafted off the shore as I cleared Selsey Bill. The shingle Bill looks flat and benign but it's beset by rocks and sandbanks, suggesting that the headland might once have extended a mile or more further out before it was eroded by the sea. The southern edge of the rocks is guarded by a red beacon, then a couple of miles further on there's a safe channel between a pair of buoys that mark some submerged sandbanks. Leaving the Sussex coast behind I negotiated the channel and set a course a little to the north of the easternmost point of the Isle of Wight, which would take me across the shipping lane called the Nab Channel and into shallower water off Bembridge. To the south sat the Nab Tower, a squat round edifice that was conceived in the 1940s as a submarine defence but built too late to see action; it now serves as a lighthouse. I crossed the channel with no problems, gave way to a tanker that was leaving its anchorage, then went on to manual steering to avoid the ferries, yachts and fishing boats that were beginning to populate the Solent.

The scene in the Solent was one of maritime busyness, with boats at anchor, yachts and dinghies trying to race in a gentle sea breeze, hovercraft and conventional ferries plying the trip to Ryde, a pair of car ferries crossing to Wootton, high-speed cat to Cowes, and the big ferries to France out of Portsmouth. A couple of freighters made their way up-Solent towards Southampton Water. Bembridge receded from view and Ryde with its long pier came abeam, then I picked a course through the slow-motion yacht races and finally through the moored boats between the two halves of Cowes. I found a quiet stretch of water to drop the mainsail, called up Cowes Yacht Haven, and tied *Indalo* to a pontoon.

Perhaps more than anywhere around the British coast Cowes is associated with yachts and sailing. The first yachting regatta was held there in 1812, there are eight yacht and sailing clubs, and the town hosts an impressive calendar of events from March to October including the Round-the-Island race in June and Cowes Week at the beginning of August. The town is familiar territory of a sort though I only visited once, four years previously when *Indalo* was still based in Poole. I'd expected the marinas to be bigger and the town to have a more exclusive feel, but there were more berths in Brighton or Eastbourne and both Dartmouth and Salcombe seem classier. But ignoring the image and the expectations that go with it Cowes is a pleasant enough place with its winding main street, its old buildings and its many nautically-themed shops. The boatyards and ferries also give it something of a working feel that was missing from my last two stops. I ate in a pub called the Waterside mainly because I'd been there before and knew it had a big window overlooking the river, then I went for a walk a little way along the Solent coast. I didn't go far, but it was the first country walk I'd had since Stonehaven.

As I returned to the boat it began to sink in that after three months of pottering from harbour to harbour I was only a few days from the end of the voyage. Cowes is a little closer to Dartmouth than Penzance is, and two fifty-mile passages would bring me home. It would be good to be back, but on the other hand it felt sad to be coming to the close of the trip. Should I run for home, or take my time and visit some of the places in between? I had no pressures either way, no crew to wait for and no real deadline other than a vague promise to my clients to be back working by the second week in September. Tomorrow I'd stay in the Isle of Wight, then I'd see how I felt and what the weather brought.

⛵

Wednesday started hot and sunny. I'd planned either to carry on down the Wight coast to Yarmouth or to explore the island by bus. The bus won, because I wanted to see something of the south-east coast which while it has some of the best coastal towns has no real harbours to speak of. The island's administrative centre and transport hub is Newport, a short bus ride from Cowes, so I could go there and then choose whether to go to the twin resorts of Sandown and Shanklin, or to Ventnor slightly further south.

The first bus to arrive went directly to Ventnor, so I hopped on that. It took a roundabout route out of Cowes and, without really getting into any open country, arrived in Newport. The island capital looked rather scruffy from what I could see, but I reminded myself that the Isle of Wight is one of the poorest parts of England. Surprising maybe for an island a stone's throw from the prosperous south coast, but it's to do with the fact that the economy is based on tourism and agriculture and a fair proportion of the work is seasonal. From Newport the bus wound, bumped and lurched its way into open countryside that began to show a more appealing side of the island. Next stop was Godshill, a twee place full of tearooms and holidaymakers and home to a model village. It looked like a model village itself. From there we continued to Ventnor, a small seaside town that starts just below the highest spot on the island, the 240m St Boniface Down, and clings on to the hillside all the way down to the sea.

Ventnor has a lively centre from where various alleyways disappear in a downward direction. I took one at random and it came out by the harbour, a recent creation to allow small craft to berth locally (though not yachts *Indalo's* size unless the skipper is feeling very adventurous and has lots of crew wielding boathooks and fenders). I walked along the sea front away from the main bathing beach and found a set of steps leading up past some chalets and beach homes, and eventually came out on a main road heading back into town. Back on the upper level I remembered that I'd spotted a place called Rex's Piano Bar from the bus, a smart-looking bistro that had a small decking terrace with views over the sea and along the beach. I didn't really want a big lunch but decided it was worth eating there if I could sit on the terrace. There was one table left, the food was good, the French waitresses were very welcoming and the view was excellent. There was a beach busy with people sunbathing and swimming, above it were terraces, greenery and the roofs of houses, and the coast in the middle distance had rocks and shingle beneath a wooded bluff. The sea was a pale blue and disappeared into haze. If I ignored some of the details I could imagine that I was soaking up the sun on the south coast of Madeira.

The bar was part of a development called Kingsview, a block of apartments that all had large sun terraces and views of the sort that I'd been enjoying. It had just won the Isle of Wight Design Award, and it seemed to be the right idea for this piece of coast given the views and the fact that Ventnor enjoys just about the warmest and sunniest climate in England. After finishing my lunch I took a short walk along one of the upper roads and through the town park, before wandering back to watch a little carnival parade and catch a very overdue bus that did the coastal circuit clockwise. I didn't see much of the coast, but did see lots of the Wight countryside: typically English rolling fields with bits of copse and hedgerow, the fields smaller than on the mainland and with more ground left wild in between. The bus stopped at Blackgang Chine, a valley in the cliffs that had been turned in to a theme park, then at a pearl shop and a couple of other places where there were lots of cars parked. Next we bumped through Freshwater and clattered along a rough road down to Alum Bay where there was a another theme park, this time for the Needles, the sea stacks off the western tip of the island. Eventually the bus rattled its way back up the road and an hour and a half after leaving Ventnor it drew into Yarmouth, where I got off.

Yarmouth was another place I'd visited in *Indalo* a few years back, but we'd arrived in fog, rowed ashore for a meal and a drink, and left early the next morning. Today the harbour was bathed in sun. It's set in a flattish landscape looking out over the Solent, and it was busy with boats as well as with day-trippers going to and fro on the ferry: a complete contrast with Ventnor. Yarmouth itself is also very different from the southern resort, being basically on the level and having much more the feel of a well-preserved village. After a wander around and a pint in one of the many pubs I caught a bus packed with people most of whom had come across on the ferry to Yarmouth or were heading back to Ryde to return home. A quick change at Newport and I was back in Cowes for the evening. Content that I'd seen two of the best bits of the Isle of Wight I had a snack on board, finished off the navigation for the morning, and turned in.

Next day my plan was to do the fifty-mile passage to Weymouth. Starting out at half-seven I would fight the tide down to Yarmouth, then pick up a fair stream to take me past the Needles and south of Bournemouth to St Alban's Head and beyond. The forecast was for a gentle to moderate westerly and possibly some rain: if conditions became too miserable I could divert to Studland and either anchor there for the night or go into Poole Harbour. Interesting though this great natural harbour is, it's not the ideal passage port because the tide runs strongly in the entrance and getting in and berthing up would represent a diversion of about ten miles each way. I'd visited Poole earlier in the year when I'd stayed at the superb new Lifeboat College for a sea safety course, and I wasn't desperate to see the place again.

The morning opened to a golden haze and even at eight when I set off the heat of the sun was making itself felt. Cowes definitely appears at its best from seaward, from the west, and beyond it the whole stretch of coast looks verdant and unspoilt. Newtown Creek comes next, once the opening to an important port until it was sacked by the French in the fourteenth century, now a National Trust nature reserve marked by a forest of yacht masts. Then Yarmouth with even more masts, just as attractive from seaward as from the shore. The tide slackened as I drew level with Yarmouth and I was soon heading past Hurst Castle on the mainland side, one of Henry VIII's fortifications against the French, and down towards the Needles.

The Needles appeared as silhouettes in the haze like dots at the end of a sentence pointing to their cousins off Studland, a reminder that these distant headlands were once joined together as part of the coast. At the end of the Needles Channel I turned west towards Anvil Point on the Dorset coast, and along with four other yachts set out across Poole Bay. The tide made short time of the crossing and soon Peveril Point appeared through the haze marking the small coastal town of Swanage, followed by the Anvil itself. The sea began to feel more disturbed and the tide whisked me along at an extra three knots, then four, then four and a half as I approached St Alban's Head. I passed the rocky bulk of St Alban's about half a mile off to keep the tide with me, as there was already a slack area inshore where some eastbound yachts were making progress unhindered. Soon afterwards a steamship loomed out of the mist, passed fairly close to port, then turned about and passed me again. There was no name on her bows but a banner on her guardrails proclaimed 'Shieldhall Open Today.' So she was the SS *Shieldhall*, one of the few steamers in service around Britain and so far as I know the only one doing regular offshore passenger trips.

Closer to Weymouth I picked up a pan-pan conversation on the radio. A motor cruiser was out on the Shambles Bank near Portland Bill for some fishing when its propellor fell off. The cruiser didn't have GPS or a hand compass and the skipper could only make a rough estimate of their position, and to complicate matters one of the crew had a medical condition and felt unwell. Portland Coastguard called out the lifeboat from Weymouth and put a helicopter on standby in case the casualty needed rapid evacuation, but a fishing boat came to the rescue and towed the cruiser towards Weymouth. From what I could hear all ended well.

Friday I spent exploring Weymouth. I'd visited twice before by sea and once to catch the ferry to Jersey, but I'd never stayed long enough to see more than the harbourside, which is probably the most interesting area anyway. The town is infamous as the place where the Black Death entered England in the fourteenth century before wiping out a third of the country's population. More happily it was promoted as a holiday resort in the 1750s by the wealthy mayor of Bath, Ralph Allen, starting its development as a seaside town. It was really put on the map though by George III, who visited thirteen times between 1789 and 1805 and had a summer palace built. Around the same time it also started to develop as a ferry port for the Channel Islands with services run by the GPO and later the Great Western steamers. Nowadays Condor have taken over with their fast catamarans, two hours to St Peter Port and three to St Helier.

My first stop was the *Shieldhall*, which had come in shortly after me and was now lying against the quay resplendent with white superstructure and green safety-painted deck. She was built in 1954 by Lobnitz of Renfrew for Glasgow City Council as a sewage-disposal boat, there being few qualms fifty years ago about dumping the waste from the city's lavatories into the sea. Although basically a coaster she was made to be a good seaworthy vessel of two hundred and sixty-eight feet and 1792 tons. Her steam engines are oil-fired, dispensing with the dirty job of shovelling coal, and they can push her along at up to sixteen knots. She operated in Glasgow until 1977 then did another eight years in Southampton for the water board before eventual rescue by a group of enthusiasts, now a charity called the Solent Steam Packet Ltd. Nowadays the *Shieldhall* does passenger trips with her crew of volunteers.

Back ashore I avoided the packed beach and had a look around the town centre, which was quite a lot bigger and better-equipped than I expected. Domestics done, I stopped off at the Royal Dorset Yacht Club for a sandwich and a drink, hoping as well to pick up some local knowledge about rounding Portland Bill. Portland is the most tidally significant headland on the English side of the Channel. Almost an island, it projects out into the Channel's stream creating a fearsome turbulence that is rough enough to be avoided in all but the calmest weather. The Bill's saving feature is that unlike the Lizard or the Cap de la Hague there are no offlying rocks and the water close to the shore is less disturbed than it is to seaward. This means that the Bill can be passed close inshore, saving the long detour to give it the recommended three to five miles' offing. Last year I did the inshore passage at neaps, but tomorrow it would be the top of springs and the pilot books advised me to take the outer route.

The yacht club was friendly and hospitable, and I soon got talking to some regulars: a mate on a Mediterranean charter yacht, an ex-merchant captain, and a single-handed yachtsman who had just completed an anticlockwise round-Britain trip in a boat similar in size to *Indalo*. They were happy enough to go inshore at any time provided the tide was with them and the wind not too strong in the opposite direction, so that was that.

After we were turned out of the club mid-afternoon I went off to see more of the town. I found a building called Brewer's Wharf on the opposite side of the harbour that houses a collection of real shops with old-style shop fronts, along with the little town museum. I nosed around in the museum and looked for information on a couple of wrecks that had intrigued me, one marked on the chart and the other com-memorated in a new-looking plaque on the quayside. The first was the original HMS *Hood*, built in 1889 to an already antiquated design because of the eponymous admiral's in-sistence on traditional, top-heavy construction. Of no value as a fighting ship by the time the first world war broke out, she was scuttled across the southern entrance of Portland harbour to thwart entry by enemy submarines. The second wreck was an unintentional one. The *Earl of Abergavenny* went down just outside Weymouth harbour in February 1805. A 1440-ton merchantman bound from London for India and China, she ran aground on the Shambles Bank, got off again, but sank within a stone's throw of safety. Over two hundred of those on board drowned including John Wordsworth, the ship's captain and younger brother of poet William.

Back on board the afternoon forecast was for north-westerlies, which would make the crossing to Dartmouth a better proposition than beating up into Lyme Bay. With my new-found local knowledge it would be possible to do it all in daylight: leave at 1030, round Portland Bill two hours later, then cross the bay carrying the tide almost all the way to arrive around half-eight in the evening. If the wind was lighter or more westerly I'd already done my homework for getting into Bridport or Lyme, so I had those options too. I could be home tomorrow, or I could take my time pottering along the Dorset and East Devon coast: Bridport, Lyme, maybe Exmouth, Torquay or Brixham, Dartmouth. I'd know when I cleared the Bill.

I left Weymouth on Saturday 20th August, day 99 of the voyage. Slipping my ropes at a quarter past ten I had a clear run out of the harbour, the morning Condor ferry already gone and the *Shieldhall* yet to depart. The sky was blue with just a few white clouds and as I cleared the breakwater I had a rare view down the Dorset coast, its cliffs lit up by the morning sun. Now part of a small flotilla I stopped the engine and set a course under sail to clear the breakwaters off Portland harbour and head for Grove Point, Portland's eastern tip. There was just enough breeze to keep up a good sailing pace and as I passed the grave of HMS *Hood* the tide turned in my favour. When the Bill came into view I began to close with the land, at 1130 passing the southern tip and its lighthouse less than a hundred metres from the shore. The sea was more agitated than it had been last time I came this way, stirred up by the wind opposing the strong current. I headed up the western side of the Bill so the tide wouldn't pull me south into Portland Race, then set the sails to come as close to the wind as I could.

On the far side of Portland the tide was slack and the wind a gentle northwesterly as predicted. My heading would take me to Torbay or maybe Teignmouth taking account of a northgoing stream at the end of the passage, but not to Lyme. Tomorrow the wind was due to turn southwesterly, so if I headed for Lyme I would have to beat against it on both days. The wind had made my decision for me, so I slackened the sails a little and set the windvane up to steer a course for Dartmouth, feeling equal measures of disappointment at missing the intermediate ports and excitement about coming home. But five miles out from the Bill the wind began to drop, and thirty minutes later I realised that my speed wasn't enough to get me into Dartmouth before dark. I started the engine, furled away the foresail, and let the autohelm take over from the windvane. There were three or four other yachts making the crossing, now with headsails furled like *Indalo*. For the moment I had little to do other than keep an eye on them and enjoy the views.

I'd crossed Lyme Bay twice before, once overnight and once in enough of a haze to hide the coast, but this time I was in luck and I had a clear view from Portland around the wide sweep of the Dorset coast and on to east Devon. Halfway across I plotted my position on exactly three degrees of longitude and made a list of bearings to ports and conspicuous features as they appeared on the chart. I took my list and a hand compass above deck, and scanned the great panorama around me. Portland fading out of view astern; Golden Cap, and then Lyme, not quite where I had expected it to be; Beer Head; Straight Point, marking the mouth of the River Exe; Hope's Nose, on the northern edge of Torbay, an indistinct smudge; Berry Head opposite it; Dartmouth, the daymark above the entrance not yet visible; and the long curve of Start Bay, a faint line on the horizon with Start Point too far away to be seen. I could sail in by eye to Dartmouth, Brixham or Torquay. Perhaps I could meet Declan and Brenda in Torquay. I tried their number, then Dec's mobile: no reply, so I kept on course for Dartmouth.

As I approached the land the cliffs between Dartmouth and Berry Head stood out, almost like an island in front of the lower land behind, and the far coast of Torbay came into view. A beam trawler was fishing a little way to the south, the beams angled up to either side making it look like a variety of aquatic insect on the water's surface. Clouds had started to gather in the sky but the sun still glinted on the sea, playing for half an hour and more like so many flashing lights, more intense as I looked towards Dartmouth as if to guide me home. A grey and black dolphin came over, barrelled underneath *Indalo* and made five half-leaps close to the bow in greeting. Then the sun lit up the coast, first with shafts of light picking out Start Bay and Dartmouth and then more fully as it came out from behind the clouds. Even the pan-pan call on the radio, where a motor cruiser had lost power off Start Point, ended happily with a tow into Salcombe. I carried the tide nearly to the craggy Mew Stone outside the mouth of the river, fought it for twenty minutes until I rounded the rocks into the Dart estuary, then picked up the flood again and let it carry *Indalo* homewards. Hoping but hardly expecting to get a walk-ashore berth on a Saturday evening in August I spotted a slightly smaller boat on the pontoon outside Dartmouth Yacht Club and made fast to it at five past seven, less than nine hours out from Weymouth. I was home.

The circumnavigation, from that cool and overcast Sunday back in mid-May when I started from Dartmouth town quay, had taken ninety-eight days and covered 1980 nautical miles over the ground, fifty less through the water as I'd had the tide with me more often than not. I'd visited sixty-five ports, harbours and anchorages and done two-thirds of the journey single-handed. It was good to be home but I felt some sadness too at having finished the trip. It was a quicker ending than I'd expected right up to the point of rounding Portland Bill, and it hadn't quite sunk in yet. Right now I needed a pint or two.

An hour later I was sitting in Bayard's Cove outside the Dartmouth Arms, the place where the *Mayflower* put in on its way to America in 1620, with a glass of Director's and a pizza on order. Appropriate in a way, as this was how I started my involvement with yachts six years before, except that we were heading out rather than coming in and this time I wasn't going to lose my dinner into the sea. I rang my parents, then Dec and Bren who were still out, then one of my other sailing friends. So nobody to welcome me back, but I wasn't sure at the moment if I wanted to celebrate or reflect.

Not that it was over yet. In the morning I needed to tidy the boat and pack away the things that were to come off. It would also be a good opportunity to walk around the town and have a proper look at the castle, which in five years of being based in the Dart I'd never been inside. After my time away Dartmouth seemed new and fresh, and I had the strange feeling of visiting a familiar place for the first time. I wanted to take in the riverside, the back streets, the church, the pubs, shops and cafés, but first stop was the castle at the river-mouth.

In fact it's three castles, all run by English Heritage. At the start of the voyage I mentioned the one built by John Hawley, but a better defence for the river was built at the end of the fifteenth century in the form of two gun towers, one either side, with a chain laid across the river bed that could be wound up to form a barrier to shipping. Unlike Saucy Mary's chain across Kyle Akin this was a real chain of metal links, and it was revived in the second world war as a submarine barrier. In 1690 a more modern gun emplacement was added to enable the more powerful cannon now available to engage ships as they approached from seaward. The emplacement was remodelled several times in each of the following three centuries, but it still housed muzzle-loading cannon until, and I find this almost incredible, 1940.

On the way back I passed what used to be the Gunfield, at One Gun Point. When I first knew Dartmouth this was a pub with regular barbecues and outdoor seating on terraces overlooking the river. In the right weather it could be an idyllic spot. It even had its own pontoon, strictly for dinghies though we tied *D'Artagnan* up there after coming back from Guernsey and sat on the terrace drinking cold beer. More recently the pub started to close for parties, and eventually it went back to being a private house. A brilliant place if you're lucky enough to live there, but a great loss if you don't: there's nowhere else on the Dart that's remotely like it. Back in town I called in at the Cherub by way of compensation, over six hundred years old and one of Dartmouth's best pubs.

After an afternoon of strolling around the town and packing things away on board, I thought I'd have a dinner worthy of marking the end of the voyage. I was late going back ashore and had reckoned without it being Sunday evening in Dartmouth in August. First choice was a place that had been called Strutt's and was now something else, to see what it was like now it had changed hands. It didn't open on a Sunday. I walked back to the river front. The restaurant above the yacht club didn't particularly appeal, and the Italian on the river front was closed. Further towards the quay the New Angel, John Burton-Race's restaurant, was also closed for the day. Upriver the Floating Bridge inn had seats on the terrace, but the evening was beginning to feel a little cool by now so I retraced my steps across town to a place called the Merchant's Table. Open, but finished serving. Finally I found an Indian restaurant which was acceptable if in my view a bit overpriced, and it didn't do sweets or coffee. Not quite the end to the day I had wanted, and back aboard the milk and yogurts had gone off so I was stuck with ship's biscuits and instant cappuccino.

Monday morning left me with just a short stretch upriver to *Indalo*'s mooring. I awoke to the sound of rain on the cabin roof, but by the time I was up it had given way to light showers and sunny spells. After getting some assistance from to move an unoccupied boat that had rafted up to me, I motored upriver. Wind and tide were against me, but I could proceed slowly and take some photographs. I passed the fuel barge and the *Res Nova*, the Dart's floating restaurant, then the rather quirky paddle-driven chain ferry or Floating Bridge. The plush Dart Marina and its nearly-finished apartments were to port, followed by the naval college's quays with their assorted vessels, and to starboard Noss Marina and Philip's former boatyard floated by. On up into the narrower part of the river past Maypool and the Greenway boathouse, past the Anchor Stone, around Greenway Quay opposite Dittisham, and into Dittisham Pool to reclaim my mooring buoy from the seaweed.

A hundred days after I had arrived on board *Indalo* had finished her voyage. All I had left to do was to write up the log , call the water taxi, and go home.

Indalo

Indalo is a Mirage 2700 yacht, sail number 220, designed by
Thames Marine and built on Canvey Island in Essex in 1986.
She was launched as a demonstration boat called *Lothlorien* in
1987 before being renamed to *Indalo* by her first owner and
berthed in West Mersea.

Her dimensions are length 8.2m (27 feet) overall, length
over deck 7.8m, waterline 6.9m, beam 2.85m, draught 1.06m.
Displacement without equipment or stores is 2.7 tonnes and
she has a ballast ratio of 48%. Her hull and deck are
fibreglass, she has twin cast-iron keels and is steered by a
tiller rather than a wheel. Her sails are a fully-battened
Bermudan (triangular) mainsail with three reefing points plus
a furling foresail, giving a basic sail area of 40m². The engine
is a Betamarine 20hp three-cylinder diesel that uses around
two litres of fuel per hour at cruising speed.

Equipment on board includes a VHF DSC radio, one fixed
and two hand-held GPS units, a Navtex receiver for weather
forecasts and navigation warnings, an echosounder, a paddle-
wheel log for measuring speed and distance through the
water, and an electronic autohelm. The windvane self-
steering gear is a direct-action model designed by Bill Belcher
and built in mahogany and marine ply by John Bennett. I hire
a liferaft for the summer and carry a selection of warning and
emergency flares.

I wear a self-inflating lifejacket with harness and safety
line, plus when single-handed a bum bag containing various
items of safety equipment: a McMurdo personal locator
beacon with its own GPS, a strobe light, safety knife, hand-

held VHF radio, whistle, signalling mirror and a pair of double-ended flares for day and night use.

Indalo can be sailed single-handed quite easily, she is ideal for two and can accommodate five at a squeeze, though for sailing I keep her maximum complement to four. She has a small galley on board with a sink, food lockers and a gas cooker, and a heads compartment with washbasin and sea toilet.

Indalo is an ancient Spanish weather-god, usually depicted as a human figure holding a rainbow between his outstretched hands as shown in a seven-thousand year old cave painting in Los Letreros in Velez Blanco. The villagers of Mojacar and the surrounding region regard the figure as a charm against storms, and he appears above doorways, in logos and on key-rings and souvenirs.

The Log

Date	Day	Leg	Passage	Naut. miles	Weather	Charts	Dist sailed	Page
14 May	1	1	Dittisham to Dartmouth	3	Rain	5602.1	3	4
15 May	2	1	Dartmouth to River Yealm	33	E 2-4 overcast	1613 5602.8	36	7
16 May	3	2	Yealm to Falmouth	44	SW 3 -> 2 then NW 3 fair	1613 1267 5602.6	80	11
17 May	4	3	Falmouth to Penzance via Newlyn	38	Little wind, fair	777 2345	118	14
25 May	12	4	Penzance to Newquay	55	S/SW 2-4, mist then fair	2345 777 1149 1168	173	24
26 May	13	5	Newquay to Padstow	17	Mizzle	1149 1168	190	27
28-29 May	15-16	6	Padstow to Dale	72	W3-4 -> NW 2 Fair	1156 C60 C13	262	30
30 May	17	7	Dale to Solva and Skomer	25	W 2-3 Fair	C13 1482 C60	287	31
31 May	18	8	Skomer to Fishguard	29	1-2 Fair	C51	316	34

Date			Route		Weather			
1 June	9	19	Fishguard to Aberystwyth	43	S 3-4 Rain	C51	359	37
5 June	10	23	Aberystwyth to Pwllheli	34	W 2-3 Fair	C51 1512	393	44
6 June	11	24	Pwllheli to Porth Nefyn	34	Var 2-3 Fair	C52 1512	427	46
7 June	12	25	Porth Nefyn to Holyhead	29	W 1-3 Fair	C52 1413	456	49
9 June	13	27	Holyhead to Port St Mary	47	NW 2-3 Fair	C62 Y70	503	53
10 June	14	28	Port St Mary to Douglas	19	E 2-3 Sunny	Y70	522	56
11 June	15	29	Douglas to Ardglass	48	NW-N 3 Fair	Y70 C62	570	58
14 June	16	32	Ardglass to Carrickfergus	41	W 2 Rain	C62 2198	611	63
15 June	17	33	Carrickfergus to Glenarm	26	Light drizzle	2198	637	68
16 June	18	34	Glenarm to Ballycastle	22	Rain	C64 2494	659	70
18 June	19	36	Ballycastle to Port Ellen	27	SE 3 Mist	2494 C64 2168	686	76
19 June	20	37	Port Ellen to Crinan	42	Mist then fair	2168 C64 2326	728	78
20 June	21	38	Crinan to Oban	24	Fair	2326 2800.3/4	752	81
22 June	22	40	Oban to Tobermory	25	SW 2-5 Fair	2800.4/5	777	85
24 June	23	42	Tobermory to Armadale	34	NE 3-5 Fair	2800.5 C66	811	89

Date	Day	Leg	Passage	Naut. miles	Weather	Charts	Dist sailed	Page
25 June	43	24	Armadale to Kyleakin via Isleornsay	20	NW 3 Fair	2208 2209	831	92
27 June	45		Moved to Kyle of Lochalsh		Fair			
28 June	46	25	Kyle of Lochalsh to Portree	21	N <2 Sunny	2209	852	98
29 June	47	26	Portree to Shieldaig	26	<2 Sunny	2209 2210	878	100
1 July	49	27	Shieldaig to Gairloch	19	SW 2-3 Fair	2210	897	104
2 July	50		Moved to Badachro	2	Fair	2210	899	
4 July	52	28	Lochinver via Gairloch	42	SW 3 or less	2210 C66 C67	941	108
5 July	53	29	Lochinver to Kinlochbervie	28	Mist	C67 2503	969	108
6 July	54	30	Kinlochbervie to Scrabster via Talmine	69	Fair	2503 C68 1462	1038	110
8 July	56	31	Scrabster to Wick	34	S 2 Fair	2162 C22 1462	1072	116
9 July	57	32	Wick to Helmsdale	29	S <2 Fair	C22 1462	1101	120
11 July	59	33	Helmsdale to Lossiemouth	30	ESE 2-3 Sunny	C22 1462	1131	123

12 July	60	34	Lossiemouth to Whitehills	24	Var 2 then NE 3-4 Fair	C22	1155	125
15 July	63	35	Whitehills to Peterhead	39	NW 2-4 Fair	C23 213	1194	128
17 July	65	36	Peterhead to Aberdeen	26	S 2-4 Fair	C23 213	1220	132
20 July	68	37	Aberdeen to Stonehaven	16	NW 3-5 Fair	C23	1236	138
22 July	70	38	Stonehaven to Arbroath	31	N-NW 3-4 Fair	C23 190	1267	141
23 July	71	39	Arbroath to Anstruther	24	E 2 Fair	190	1291	143
24 July	72	40	Anstruther to Eyemouth	31	NE 2-3 Fair	C27 160 1612	1322	145
25 July	73	41	Eyemouth to Berwick-upon-Tweed	11	N 2 Fair	160 1612	1333	148
27 July	75	42	Berwick to North Shields	56	S/SE 2 Fair	C24 156	1389	153
29 July	77	43	North Shields to Sunderland	11	NE 1 Fog	152	1400	158
31 July	79	44	Sunderland to Hartlepool	21	N 4-5 Fair	C24	1421	161
1 Aug	80	45	Hartlepool to Whitby	25	N 1-2 Fair	C24 1612	1446	163
2 Aug	81	46	Whitby to Bridlington via Filey	40	Var 3 or less Fair	C29	1486	165
3 Aug	82	47	Bridlington to Grimsby	48	SW/W 3-7 Fair	C29 109	1534	167

Date	Day	Leg	Passage	Naut. miles	Weather	Charts	Dist sailed	Page
5 Aug	84	48	Grimsby to Wells-next-the-Sea	57	SW/NW 2 Fair	109 C29 Y9	1591	172
6 Aug	85	49	Wells to Lowestoft	59	W-NW-N 3 Fair	Y9 C28 1570	1650	175
8 Aug	87	50	Lowestoft to Shotley	45	NW 3-4 Shs	C28 2400.4	1695	177
9 Aug	88		Moved to Harwich via Levington	7	Var 2 Fair		1702	
10 Aug	89	51	Harwich to Ramsgate	44	Var 2 Fair	C1 C8	1746	181
11 Aug	90	52	Ramsgate to Dover	17	S 0-2 Fair	C8	1763	185
12 Aug	91	53	Dover to Eastbourne	47	NW 2-4 Fair	C8	1810	188
15 Aug	94	54	Eastbourne to Brighton	22	NW 2-3 Fair	C9	1832	193
16 Aug	95	55	Brighton to Cowes	48	Var 0-2 Sunny	C9 5600.3/11	1880	196
18 Aug	97	56	Cowes to Weymouth	49	Var 0-2 Haze	5600.2/4 5601.4/5/7	1929	200
20 Aug	99	57	Weymouth to Dartmouth	53	NW 2-3 Fair	5601.1/4/7 5602.1	1982	205
22 Aug	101		Dartmouth to Dittisham	3	Fair with shs	5602.1	1985	